a JOKE book for kids

awesome JOKE book for kids

ARCTURUS

ARCTURUS
This edition published in 2008 by Arcturus Publishing Limited
26/27 Bickels Yard, 151–153 Bermondsey Street,
London SE1 3HA

ISBN: 978-1-84837-173-6

Illustrations by Peter Coupe

Printed in Singapore

Contents...

STUPID SCHOOLDAYS

Why did the maths teacher take a ruler in his car ?

So he could see how long it took him to get to work in the morning !

★

I hope you aren't going to spend the whole lesson watching the clock !

Certainly not, Sir. I have my alarm set for 3.45, and I'm hoping to get a little nap later !

★

What do you shout when Santa Claus does the register ?

Present !

I thought you were going to play school with me today !

I did - I decided to play absent !

★

What do you do if someone faints in a maths exam ?

Try to bring them 2 !

★

Parent - Why have you given my little boy such a bad report ? He's as intelligent as the next boy !

Teacher - Yes, but the next boy is an idiot !

★

Why are you taking that sponge into your lesson ?

I always find History such an absorbing subject !

★

Did you hear about the maths teacher who was thrown out of the pizza restaurant ? He asked how long his pizza would be !

Vicar - Can anyone tell me what Samson did for a living ?

Pupil - I think he was a comedian -
it says in the Bible that he
brought the house down !

★

Why does your teacher have her hair in a bun ?

Because she has a face like a burger !

★

Why do teachers never marry dairy farmers ?

They are like chalk and cheese !

★

Why do doctors enjoy their schooldays ?

Because they are good at examinations !

★

So, Jessica, you claim to know all your tables -
let's hear them then !

Dining room table, kitchen table, living room table...

COLLECTIVE NOUNS....

A NUMBER of maths teachers !

A BAKE of cookery teachers !

A TEAM of P.E. teachers !

A CONCENTRATION of science teachers !

A BAND of music teachers !

A FOREST of woodwork teachers !

A BANK of economics teachers !

A SCHOOL of headteachers !

Teacher - Sally, give me a sentence with the word 'aroma' in it !

Sally - My uncle Fred is always travelling, he's aroma !

★

What did the ghostly music teacher play ?

Haunting melodies !

★

Why do vampire teachers not like computers ?

They hate anything new fangled !

★

The maths teacher is feeling run down today !

Wow ! Did anyone get the number of the car that did it ?

★

What happens to a maths teacher's class when he retires ?

Before or after you've woken them up ?

SCHOOL LIBRARY - NEW BOOKS

The Haunted House
by
Hugo First !

The Broken Window
by
Eva Brickatit !

The Filthy Chinese Farmhouse
by
Who Flung Dung !

The Hungry Man
by
Edna Breakfast !

★

Now - just settle down you lot ! I don't come into this classroom to listen to this sort of racket !

Oh - where do you usually go, Miss ?

★

When does Mother Nature need a pencil ?

When the winter nights start drawing in !

I call my first year class my little treasures - because goodness only knows where they were dug up!

★

Why do history teachers like fruit cake?

Because it's full of dates!

★

Headteacher - Mr Phelps, do you have any sawdust?

Mr Phelps - No, all my dust is perfectly healthy thank you!

Why are you scratching yourself boy ?

Because no-one else knows where I itch !

★

Teacher - Name two days of the week starting with T.

Pupil - Today and tomorrow !

★

Teacher - Clark, have you been an idiot all your life ?

Clark - Not yet, Sir !

★

Pupil - I got in trouble at school today
for something I didn't do.

Parent - What was it ?

Pupil - My homework !

★

Have you heard about the cross-eyed teacher ?

She couldn't control her pupils !

John - what is the plural of 'baby'?

Twins!

★

Give me a sentence with the word 'politics' in it!

Our parrot swallowed the alarm clock, and now politics!

★

In the Bible it tells us that God was a healer!

I know that, Sir, because he gave Moses some tablets!

If you multiply 245 by 3456 and divide the answer by 165, then subtract 752, what will you get ?

The wrong answer, Miss !

★

What's the difference between a train and a teacher ?

A train says "choo - choo" but a teacher says "take that gum out of your mouth this instant !"

★

Why did the scruffy schoolboy finally take a bath ?

Because he realised that grime doesn't pay !

★

Johnson - Your parents are multi-millionaires and yet you still smell awful !

That's because we're filthy rich, Miss !

★

Inspector - How many teachers work in this school ?

Pupil - Very few !

How do you make a sick insect better ?

Give it a 'T', then it will be a stick insect !

★

Why does the music teacher need a ladder ?

To reach the high notes !

★

What do history teachers do before they get married ?

They go out on dates !

★

Who teaches all the boys called Ed ?

The Ed teacher !

I didn't use a recipe for this casserole -
I made it out of my own head!

I thought it tasted of sawdust!

★

Why are you always late for school?

Because I threw my alarm clock in the bin!

Why on earth did you do that?

It kept going off when I was asleep
and kept waking me up!

★

Where do vampire schoolchildren go for field trips?

Lake Eerie!

★

My maths teacher is a real peach!

You mean she's pretty?

No - I mean she has a heart of stone!

Matheson, where is Turkey ?

No idea, Sir, we threw ours away after Christmas !

★

I think our school must be haunted - because our teacher keeps going on about the school spirit !

★

Evans, are you any good at History ?

Well, Miss, to be honest, yes and no !

What do you mean yes and no ?

I mean, yes, I'm no good at History !

Maths teacher - If there were a dozen sheep and six jumped over the fence, how many would be left ?

Pupil - None, Sir !

Maths teacher - Oh, dear, I'm afraid you don't know much about maths do you ?

Pupil - And you don't know much about sheep. If one goes, they all go !

★

Why did the teacher pick Davies to be teacher's pet ?

Because he is the person who looks most like her dog !

★

I'm sorry Mr Cyclops, I don't think you are suited to teaching - you only have the one pupil !

★

You had better behave in Mr Simkins' music class or you'll find yourself in treble !

What do elves learn at school ?

The elf-abet !

★

What sort of vampire is attracted to music and soldiers ?

A sharp major !

★

What kind of boat do smart kids travel on !

Scholar - ships !

★

Why did the music teacher ban skeletons from keyboard lessons ?

They have no organs !

★

Why is that boy locked up in a cage in the corner of the classroom ?

Oh, he's the teacher's pet !

Please, Miss, I've swallowed my pencil sharpener!

You must be choking!

No, Miss, I'm perfectly serious!

★

This school pie has hairs in it!

That's odd – it says rabbit pie on the menu!

★

What did one pencil say to the other pencil?

Whoa, you're looking sharp today!

There once was a schoolboy called Pete,

Who stuck coloured pens on his feet.

Now wherever he goes,

If he wiggles his toes,

He can draw, on the floor - now that's neat !

★

Rodrick, how would you address a Dutchman and his twin brother ?

In double Dutch, Miss !

★

My little Ben is doing so well at school, he can speak three languages fluently - double dutch, complete twaddle and utter gibberish !

★

What do you get if you look at a vampire teacher through a telescope ?

A horrorscope !

Why was the teacher chased by a hen?

It was after his wages - he said he got paid chicken feed!

★

How does a maths teacher remove hard wax from his ears?

He works it out with his pencil!

★

Teacher – Smith, you've been playing with that blotting paper the whole lesson - you obviously find it very absorbing!

Brown, name five things that contain milk!

Yogurt, cheese and 3 cows!

★

My Brian is very quick at picking up music – they always send for him when they want to move the school piano!

★

Now, for your Art homework I want you to draw a self portrait!

Does it matter who it's a portrait of, Miss?

★

How did people react when electricity was first discovered?

They got a nasty shock!

★

How did people react when gas was first used to heat homes?

Most people were happy, but one or two people were a bit sniffy about it!

Why is Woods at the hospital today?

Because we had to change lessons yesterday!

How on earth can that injure anyone?

Well, we usually have cookery - but it was changed to chemistry - and Woods always licks the spoon!

★

What is an alkali?

When a drunk person tells you something that isn't true!

Why did the music teacher tell his pupil to beat it ?

He was teaching him to play the drum !

★

What sort of music makes a teacher take his shoes off ?

Soul music !

★

Why was the music teacher locked out of his classroom ?

His keys were in the piano !

★

What is the first thing teachers at the Frankenstein school do every morning ?

They go into assembly !

★

How did your mum know you hadn't washed your face this morning ?

I forgot to wet the soap !

Is the maths teacher in a good mood today?

I wouldn't count on it!

★

Did you hear about the ex maths teacher who worked on the stock exchange? He was divided about whether to buy additional shares or take away his profits!

★

What class did the new robot teacher get on his first day?

The bottom class...he got all the nuts!

What do they have for lunch at the monster school?

Boiled legs and pickled bunions!

★

What does the robot teacher's mum do
for a living?

She's a washer woman!

★

How can you tell when a robot teacher
is going mad?

He goes screwy!

★

Please French teacher,

Listen to me,

I don't know the French,

But I really need a oui!

One in three people are stupid - so have a good look at two of your classmates. If they seem OK then it's probably you !

★

Pupil – I always come out in spots when I'm doing a maths exam !

Friend – Sounds like a bad case of decimals !

★

I sprained my ankle and had to miss Games for two weeks !

Lucky you ! Our sports teacher never accepts a lame excuse for missing games !

★

The school dinners here are untouched by human hand - there's a gorilla in the kitchen !

★

Teacher – When I was your age I thought nothing of walking 5 miles to school.

Pupil – I agree, I don't think much of it either!

Did you hear about the Spanish teacher who broke his leg but was back at work two hours later?

He made a maracas recovery!

★

I couldn't do my homework last night because my pen ran out, and I'm not allowed to go out of the house after dark!

★

Williams, what is the covering of a tree trunk called?

Don't know, Sir!

Bark, Williams, Bark!

Woof, woof!

★

It's a good job your name is Mark – because you certainly don't seem able to get any in your exams!

When did early people start wearing clothes?

In the Iron Age!

★

Sir, what would I have to write to pass my exams?

Someone else's name at the top of
your exam paper!

★

Why did 1920s gangsters in America carry
musical instrument cases?

Because they committed robbery with violins!

★

Can anyone tell me which is the longest night
of the year?

Yes, Miss, a fortnight!

★

Why did the teacher put the lights on?

Because the class was so dim!

What happens to children who misbehave at magic school ?

They are ex - spelled !

★

Mr Jones, I really think your daughter needs an encyclopedia for school !

Why can't she walk like all her friends ?

★

Smith - why weren't you here at 8.45 this morning ?

Because I was held up by that sign outside - it says 'Slow, school ahead' !

We're studying Byron in English class !

What was he famous for ?

I think he invented the ball point pen !

★

What is the plural of mouse ?

Mice !

What is the plural of house ?

Hice !

★

If we do the 10 times table, 10 times,
how many times will we have done it ?

Is it a trick question ?

★

Where do skinny teachers train ?

Puny - versity !

Where do crazy teachers train?

Loony - versity!

★

Where do alien teachers train?

Moony - versity!

★

Where do music teachers train?

Tuney - versity!

Did you hear about the school cleaner who married a history teacher ?

He was brushing up on some old dates and he swept her off her feet !

★

Teacher – Joe, how can you work out the age of a tree frog?

Joe – Cut it in half and count the rings ?

★

Violin for sale - going cheap - no strings attached !

★

"Good morning class," said the vampire English teacher. "Today we will learn the alphabat !"

★

The teachers have been working flat out in the staff room, marking exam papers !

Really ? I thought they were asleep as usual !

How can a school cook also be a history teacher ?

They know more than anyone else
about ancient grease !

★

Why are school singing classes like someone
locked out of their house ?

Because neither of them can find the right key !

★

Smith - how do you feel about H G Wells ?

No, idea, Sir, we get all our water from a tap !

FOR SALE - MUSIC TEACHER RETIRING

One piano complete with stool, sheet music and earplugs!

★

Why did Catherine of Aragon marry Henry VIII?

She was told she needed a ruler to help her with her maths exam!

★

Where does the vampire teacher's girlfriend work?

In the class necks to his!

★

Do your pupils miss you?

No, that's why I've got this bruise on my forehead!

★

Do you think my son has what it takes to be a pilot?

Well - he certainly spends plenty of time with his head in the clouds!

What happens to old maths teachers ?

They are taken away !

★

What happens when music teachers are sick?

They send in a note !

★

What happens to old history teachers ?

They reach their best before date !

★

What happens to old French teachers ?

One day they realise that un oeuf is enough !

Does your father still help you with your homework?

No, Miss, I can get it wrong all on my own now!

★

Why does this class keep shouting "Miss, Miss, Miss" when you know very well that your teacher is a married woman?

Because she keeps dodging the stuff we throw at her!

★

Well, son, how did you find your geography exam?

With a map and compass, how else!

★

Why is the history teacher all dressed up in a suit and tie?

No idea - maybe he has an important date!

★

How do you get straight As?

By using a ruler!

What's the worst thing you're likely to find in the school cafeteria?

The food!

★

Why did the vampire hate school on Tuesdays?

Because that was the day they had steak for school dinners!

★

Today is flying saucer day in the school cafeteria – because of the unidentified frying objects!

A SCHOOLTEACHER'S FAVOURITE THINGS...

Book The Caine Mutiny!

Film Rain Man (because then they cancel Games!)

Actor Michael Caine!

Saying Absence makes the heart grow fonder!

★

Did you hear about the science teacher who was always playing tricks on people? He was a real particle joker!

★

Did you hear about the geography teacher who mapped out his career?

Or the archaeology teacher whose job was in ruins?

★

What musical instrument does the school cat play?

A mouse organ!

What kind of meals do maths teachers eat ?

Square meals !

★

Teacher - Who built the ark ?

Pupil - Noah idea !

★

Lewis - What do you get if you drop a
piano down a mineshaft ?

A flat minor !

★

Did you hear about the school Head who gave a
pupil some lines for the first time in his career ?

It was head line news !

★

If you want to test the theory about a link
between television and violence...try telling your
maths teacher that you sat and watched television
all night instead of doing your homework !

Jones, how many times have I told you not to eat sweets in class ?

Six, Miss !

Rather more than six I think, young man !

Yes, but that's as far as I can count !

★

Hamilton, I think you need glasses !

What makes you think that, Sir ?

You're facing the wrong way !

Elliott, have you ever hunted bear ?

No Sir, but I've been fishing in a pair of swimming trunks !

★

Does anyone know why the Romans built straight roads ?

Yes, Sir, because they didn't have steering wheels on their chariots !

★

Our school dinners are full of iron - which is probably why they are so difficult to chew !

★

Teacher - Which birds are found in Portugal ?

Pupil - Portugeese !

★

What did you get for Christmas ?

A mouth organ - it's the best present I've ever had because my mum gives me extra pocket money every week not to play it !

KNOCK, KNOCK

Knock, Knock !
Who's there ?
Justin
Justin who ?
Justin time to let me in !

★

Knock, Knock !
Who's there ?
Anna
Anna who ?
Anna noying habit of yours, locking the door like this !

★

Knock, Knock !
Who's there ?
Josie
Josie who ?
Josie anyone else out here ?

★

Knock, Knock !
Who's there ?
Paula
Paula who ?
Paula door open and you'll see !

Knock, Knock!
Who's there?
Annette
Annette who?
Annette Curtain!

★

Knock, Knock!
Who's there?
Angus
Angus who?
Angus me coat up and put the kettle on!

Knock, Knock !
Who's there ?
Elvis
Elvis who ?
Elvis is a turn up for the books !

★

Knock, Knock !
Who's there ?
Alma
Alma who ?
Alma time seems to be spent on this doorstep !

★

Knock, Knock !
Who's there ?
Fletch
Fletch who ?
Fletch a bucket of water, your house is on fire !

★

Knock, Knock !
Who's there ?
Phil
Phil who ?
Phil this cup with sugar would you, I've run out !

Knock, Knock!
Who's there?
Homer
Homer who?
Homer goodness, I've come to the wrong house!

★

Knock, Knock!
Who's there?
Alex
Alex who?
Alex the way you've done the garden!

★

Knock, Knock!
Who's there?
Chas
Chas who?
Chas pass the key through the letter box
and I'll open the door myself!

Knock, Knock !
Who's there ?
Mo
Mo who ?
Mo than you'll ever know !

★

Knock, Knock !
Who's there ?
Matt
Matt who ?
Matt as well settle down, looks like I'm in for a long wait !

★

Knock, Knock !
Who's there ?
Jester
Jester who ?
Jester day, all my troubles seemed so far away... !

★

Knock, Knock !
Who's there ?
A. Lister
A. Lister who ?
A. Lister good reasons why you should open the door !

Knock, Knc
Who's there
Zeb
Zeb who ?
Zeb better be a good reason f
me waiting out here !

★

Knock, Knock !
Who's there ?
Greta
Greta who ?
Greta friend like that again, and you'll end up with none at all !

★

Knock, Knock !
Who's there ?
Paul
Paul who ?
Paul the door open for goodness sake !

★

Knock, Knock !
Who's there ?
Will
Will who ?
Will I have to wait much longer ?

Knock, Knock!
Who's there?
Woody
Woody who?
Woody open the door if we asked him nicely?

★

Knock, Knock!
Who's there?
Kline
Kline who?
Kline of you to invite me round!

★

Knock, Knock!
Who's there?
Polly
Polly who?
Polly door handle again, I think it's just stiff!

Knock, Knock!
Who's there?
Keith
Keith who?
Keith your hands where I can see them!

★

Knock, Knock!
Who's there?
Imogen
Imogen who?
Imogen you were out here...

★

Knock, Knock!
Who's there?
India
India who?
India is some of my stuff and I've come to collect it!

★

Knock, Knock!
Who's there?
Kat
Kat who?
Kat you again?

Knock, Knock!
Who's there?
Honor Claire
Honor Claire who?
Honor Claire day you can see forever...!

★

Knock, Knock!
Who's there?
Alvin
Alvin who?
Alvin your heart - just you vait and see!

★

Knock, Knock!
Who's there?
Tom
Tom who?
Tom to the window and have a look!

Knock, Knock!
Who's there?
Candy
Candy who?
Candy owner of this big red car come and move it off my drive!

★

Knock, Knock!
Who's there?
Alfie
Alfie who?
Alfie good to see you again!

★

Knock, Knock!
Who's there?
Kim
Kim who?
Kim just too late to see you!

★

Knock, Knock!
Who's there?
Adair
Adair who?
Adair you to guess!

Knock, Knock !
Who's there ?
Chuck
Chuck who ?
Chuck the key under the door and I'll let myself in !

★

Knock, Knock !
Who's there ?
Khan
Khan who ?
Khan you give me a lift to school ?

★

Knock, Knock !
Who's there ?
Mavis
Mavis who ?
Mavis be the last time you keep me waiting !

★

Knock, Knock !
Who's there ?
Darren
Darren who ?
Darren nother excuse to keep me out here ?

Knock, Knock!
Who's there?
Luke
Luke who?
Luke through the letterflap and you'll see!

★

Knock, Knock!
Who's there?
Colin
Colin who?
Colin in for a chat!

★

Knock, Knock!
Who's there?
Wendy
Wendy who?
Wendy you want me to call round again?

Knock, Knock !
Who's there ?
Joanna
Joanna who ?
Joanna have a guess ?

★

Knock, Knock !
Who's there ?
Trudy
Trudy who ?
Trudy my word I've come to collect you !

★

Knock, Knock !
Who's there ?
Trish
Trish who ?
Bless you !

Knock, Knock !
Who's there ?
Wallace
Wallace who ?
Wallace is a fine how do you do... !

★

Knock, Knock !
Who's there ?
I Know Kung fu
I Know Kung fu who ?
I'd better not upset you then !

★

Knock, Knock !
Who's there ?
Cohen
Cohen who ?
Cohen to knock just once more, then I'm going away !

★

Knock, Knock !
Who's there ?
Kent
Kent who ?
Kent you stop asking questions and open the door ?

Knock, Knock !
Who's there ?
Alan
Alan who ?
Alan 'nounce myself once you've opened the door ! !

★

Knock, Knock !
Who's there ?
Carter
Carter who ?
Carter stray dog - is it yours ?

★

Knock, Knock !
Who's there ?
Karl
Karl who ?
I'll Karl again another day !

★

Knock, Knock !
Who's there ?
Ahmed
Ahmed who ?
Ahmed a big mistake coming here !

Knock, Knock !
Who's there ?
Ginger
Ginger who ?
Ginger hear the doorbell ?

★

Knock, Knock !
Who's there ?
Courtney
Courtney who ?
Courtney door, can you open it and set me free ?

★

Knock, Knock !
Who's there ?
Isabelle
Isabelle who ?
Isabelle not working ?

Knock, Knock !
Who's there ?
Eeny Minnie
Eeny Minnie who ?
Eeny Minnie Miny Mo !

★

Knock, Knock !
Who's there ?
Guess Simon
Guess Simon who ?
Guess Simon the wrong doorstep !

★

Knock, Knock !
Who's there ?
Wendy
Wendy who ?
Wendy red, red robin comes bob,
bob bobbin' along, along...

★

Knock, Knock !
Who's there ?
Sid
Sid who ?
Sid you'd be ready to go at three o'clock !

Knock, Knock!
Who's there?
Amos
Amos who?
Amos quito is chasing me – please let me in!

★

Knock, Knock!
Who's there?
Arnie
Arnie who?
Arnie ever going to let me in?

★

Knock, Knock!
Who's there?
Ken
Ken who?
Ken you come out to play?

★

Knock, Knock!
Who's there?
Wendy
Wendy who?
Wendy come to collect the rent, I'm off!

Knock, Knock !
Who's there ?
Seymour
Seymour who ?
Seymour of me by opening the door !

★

Knock, Knock !
Who's there ?
Sid
Sid who ?
Sid down and I'll explain !

★

Knock, Knock !
Who's there ?
Charlie
Charlie who ?
Charlie you know the sound of my voice by now !

★

Knock, Knock !
Who's there ?
Hedda
Hedda who ?
Hedda nough of this – I'm off !

Knock, Knock !
Who's there ?
Ivan
Ivan who ?
Ivan idea you're going to keep me waiting out here !

★

Knock, Knock !
Who's there ?
Gin
Gin who ?
Gin know how cold it is out here !

★

Knock, Knock !
Who's there ?
Farmer
Farmer who ?
Farmer distance your house looks much bigger !

Knock, Knock !
Who's there ?
Linda
Linda who ?
Linda hand to get this heavy suitcase up the steps !

★

Knock, Knock !
Who's there ?
Tex
Tex who ?
Tex you ages to open the door !

★

Knock, Knock !
Who's there ?
Hardy
Hardy who ?
Hardy har, fooled you !

★

Knock, Knock !
Who's there ?
Yul
Yul who ?
Yul soon see !

Knock, Knock!
Who's there?
Courtney
Courtney who?
Courtney good football matches lately?

★

Knock, Knock!
Who's there?
Mary
Mary who?
Mary Christmas, ho, ho, ho!

Knock, Knock !
Who's there ?
Carla
Carla who ?
Carla taxi, I'm leaving !

★

Knock, Knock !
Who's there ?
Giraffe
Giraffe who ?
Giraffe to ask me that stupid question ?

★

Knock, Knock !
Who's there ?
Paul
Paul who ?
Paul the other one !

★

Knock, Knock !
Who's there ?
Ringo
Ringo who ?
Ringo, ringo roses... !

Knock, Knock !
Who's there ?
Mike
Mike who ?
Mike your mind up !

★

Knock, Knock !
Who's there ?
Spock
Spock who ?
Spock the difference between me and my twin brother !

★

Knock, Knock !
Who's there ?
Teacher
Teacher who ?
Teacher self for a few days. I'm off on holiday !

Knock, Knock !
Who's there ?
Tessa
Tessa who ?
Tessa long time for you to open the door !

★

Knock, Knock !
Who's there ?
Carl
Carl who ?
Carl round to my house and I won't keep you waiting !

★

Knock, Knock !
Who's there ?
You
You who ?
Hello !

★

Knock, Knock !
Who's there ?
Simon
Simon who ?
Simon every occasion - you always make me wait !

Knock, Knock !
Who's there ?
Wade
Wade who ?
Wade a minute I'll just check !

★

Knock, Knock !
Who's there ?
Morgan
Morgan who ?
Morgan you could ever imagine !

★

Knock, Knock !
Who's there ?
Jacqueline
Jacqueline who ?
Jacqueline Hyde !!

Knock, Knock !
Who's there ?
Callista
Callista who ?
Callista warm reception I was expecting ?

★

Knock, Knock !
Who's there ?
Teresa
Teresa who ?
Teresa jolly good fellow !

★

Knock, Knock !
Who's there ?
Mouse
Mouse who ?
Mouse get a key of my own !

★

Knock, Knock !
Who's there ?
Batman
Batman who ?
You mean there's more than one ?

Knock, Knock!
Who's there?
Donna
Donna who?
Donna knock once more then I'm going home!

★

Knock, Knock!
Who's there?
Egbert
Egbert who?
Egbert no bacon!

★

Knock, Knock!
Who's there?
Misty
Misty who?
Misty door bell again!

★

Knock, Knock!
Who's there?
Lester
Lester who?
Lester do out here than in there!

Knock, Knock !
Who's there ?
Just Paul
Just Paul who ?
Just Pauling your leg – it's Steve really !

★

Knock, Knock !
Who's there ?
Fitz
Fitz who ?
Fitz not too much trouble, can you please open the door ?

★

Knock, Knock !
Who's there ?
Major
Major who ?
Major mind up to open the door yet ?

★

Knock, Knock !
Who's there ?
Mandy
Mandy who ?
Mandy lifeboats !

Knock, Knock!
Who's there?
Belle
Belle who?
Belle don't work, so I'm having to knock!

★

Knock, Knock!
Who's there?
Alex
Alex who?
Alex to knock on doors and run away!

Knock, Knock !
Who's there ?
Vance
Vance who ?
Vance more I knock on your door in the dead of night !

★

Knock, Knock !
Who's there ?
Yootha
Yootha who ?
Yootha person with the second-hand cooker for sale ?

★

Knock, Knock !
Who's there ?
Ozzie
Ozzie who ?
Ozzie Modo !

★

Knock, Knock !
Who's there ?
Chester
Chester who ?
Chester minute – I'm on the wrong street !

Knock, Knock !
Who's there ?
Carl
Carl who ?
Carl this a friendly greeting ? I don't !

★

Knock, Knock !
Who's there ?
Mustapha
Mustapha who ?
Mustapha good reason to keep me waiting !

★

Knock, Knock !
Who's there ?
Willy
Willy who ?
Willy hurry up and let me in !

Knock, Knock !
Who's there ?
Posh
Posh who ?
Posh the door open and you'll see !

★

Knock, Knock !
Who's there ?
Baby
Baby who ?
Baby I shouldn't hab come round wiv dis cold !

★

Knock, Knock !
Who's there ?
Fred
Fred who ?
Fred you'll have to let me in !

★

Knock, Knock !
Who's there ?
Russell
Russell who ?
Russell up a nice hot cup of tea –
it's freezing out here !

Knock, Knock!
Who's there?
Homer
Homer who?
Homer goodness – I can't remember myself!

★

Knock, Knock!
Who's there?
Bart
Bart who?
Bart time you opened this door!

★

Knock, Knock!
Who's there?
Denise
Denise who?
Denise are cold – let me in!

Knock, Knock !
Who's there ?
May
May who ?
May I come in ?

★

Knock, Knock !
Who's there ?
Lass
Lass who ?
How long have you been a cowboy ?

★

Knock, Knock !
Who's there ?
Doctor
Doctor who ?
No, Doctor Smith - you sent for me because you have the flu !

★

Knock, Knock !
Who's there ?
Jerome
Jerome who ?
Jerome at last !

Knock, Knock !
Who's there ?
Giselle
Giselle who ?
Giselle flowers in there ?

★

Knock, Knock !
Who's there ?
Will
Will who ?
Will wait out here until you let us in !

★

Knock, Knock !
Who's there ?
Jaffa
Jaffa who ?
Jaffa keep me waiting ?

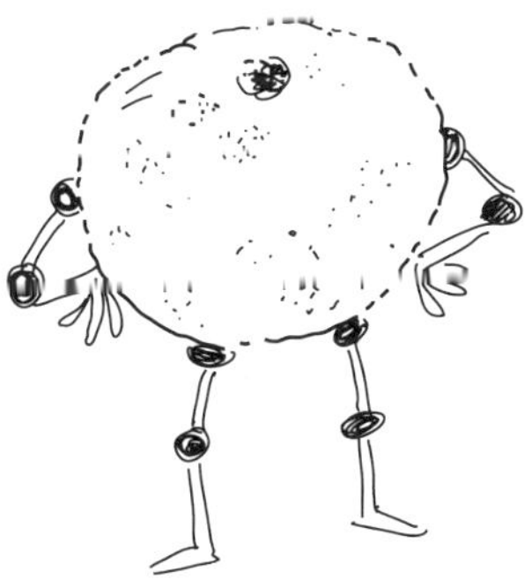

Knock, Knock !
Who's there ?
Our Tell
Our Tell who ?
Our Tell you what I want, what I really really want... !

★

Knock, Knock !
Who's there ?
Terminator
Terminator who ?
Terminator sandwiches early, so she sent me to get some more !

★

Knock, Knock !
Who's there ?
Red
Red who ?
Red your letters, you can have them back now !

★

Knock, Knock !
Who's there ?
Walter
Walter who ?
Walter strange thing to ask !

SPOOKY STUFF

What do they sing in the vampire version of Abba?

"Fang you for the music!"

★

How do monsters write letters?

With fountain men!

★

Why do monster mums and dads tell their children to eat cabbage?

Because they want them to have a healthy green complexion!

★

Why did the ghost get the job?

Because he was clearly superior!

★

Did you hear about the giant monster who took a hump-back in a plastic box to work with him?

It was his packed hunch!

What did the monster get when he fell through a window ?

A pane !

★

Should baby monsters eat humans on an empty stomach ?

No, they should eat them on a plate like everyone else !

★

Why did the zombie go to the chemist ?

He wanted something to help stop his coffin !

★

What is the first thing you should put into a haunted house ?

Someone else !

★

What do they employ in monster hospitals ?

A skeleton staff !

Baby monster - When I grow up I want to drive a tank !

Mummy monster - Well, I certainly won't stand in your way !

★

Why was the monster called Porridge ?

Because he was grey and thick !

★

What should you do after shaking hands with a monster ?

Count your fingers !

★

What is a monster's favourite game ?

Squash !

★

Did you hear about the zombie who was having a party ? He didn't know how many people would be coming...it depended on who he could dig up !

What did the blacksmith do when he saw Frankenstein's neck ?

He made a bolt for it !

★

How did the fruit bats go into Noah's Ark ?

In pears !

★

Did the computerised monster have any brothers ?

No, but he had hundreds of tran - sisters !

How do slimy monsters fight ?

They just slug it out !

★

Why did Dracula visit a psychiatrist ?

He thought he was going batty !

★

Why do vampires go to lots of pop concerts ?

They love being in fang clubs !

How did you know I was a ghost ?

Oh, I can see right through you !

★

When a vampire drinks too much, what does he get ?

A fangover !

★

Why do sausages and bacon spit when they are being cooked ?

Because it's a terror-frying experience !

★

What did King Tutankhamen hate most of all ?

Having to go shopping with his mummy !

★

Why was the mummy covered in gold and silver bandages with big bows ?

It was his Christmas wrapping !

Did you hear about the mummy who wanted to be a rock star?

He started his own rock bandage!

★

What do ghostly policemen do?

They haunt down criminals!

★

What do you call a friendly mummy?

A chummy!

★

Did you hear about the werewolf who dropped his trousers?

Well – it was a full moon!

How do you scare vampires ?

Ask if they would like a little garlic with their steak !

★

How does a vampire lock his coffin ?

With skeleton keys !

★

Did you hear about the overweight Scandinavian cannibal ?

He was always eating Swedes between meals !

★

How do monsters eat their dinner ?

They wolf it down !

★

Why was the vampire's bank account always in the red ?

Because it was in a blood bank !

Why did one skeleton tell the other one off ?

Because he had been telling fibulas !

★

What sort of monster lives in a tissue ?

A bogeyman !

★

What do ghosts eat for dinner ?

Spook - ghetti !

★

Why does the monster shop at the sewage works ?

He likes convenience food !

★

What is the first thing a monster eats in a restaurant ?

The waiter !

"Hurry up," said the father skeleton to his son, "or you'll be late for the skull bus!"

★

What sort of horses do monsters ride?

Night mares!

★

What does a monster call knights in armour?

Tinned food!

★

What do vampires eat for lunch?

Fangers and mash!

What did the monster say when he threw a human into a pit of werewolves ?

"Looks like you're going to the dogs !"

★

Why is the tribe of Bolog now extinct ?

Because monsters used to eat lots of spaghetti with Bolog knees !

★

Where did the vampire go on his holiday in China ?

Fang - Hi !

★

Why are vampires good at treating people with coughs and colds ?

Because they can clear your throat in seconds !

★

Why do vampires like runners ?

They adore fast food !

Why is monster coffee so noisy ?

Because they like scream in it !

★

What is the shortest party game that monsters know ?

Swallow the leader !

★

Why do ghosts make good fashion models ?

Because no matter what they are wearing
they always look so ghoul !

What do you call a pair of ghostly glasses ?

Spectre - cles !

★

Who do you take to a vampire party ?

The girl necks door !

★

How did the ghostly teacher make sure his pupils had learned what he had written on the blackboard ?

He went through it again !

What do you call a James Bond monster ?

Ghoul finger !

★

How do two monsters decide who owns something ?

They fright each other for it !

★

How do vampires try out a new blood group ?

They suck it and see !

★

How do vampires get clean ?

In a blood bath !

★

What do you call a vampire with no tooth ?

Pointless !

What noise do baby witches make when
they are playing with toy cars ?

Broom, broom !

★

What kind of street does a ghost like best?

A dead end !

★

Why was the stone monster always short of money ?

He was always hard up !

★

What do you call a kind, helpful monster who
likes flowers and butterflies ?

A failure !

★

What fictional character are werewolves afraid of ?

Long John Silver !

Who do vampires invite to their weddings?

All their blood relatives!

★

Why do ghosts never feel guilty?

They have a clear conscience!

★

What do you call a vampire that you can dip into your tea?

Count Dunkula!

Why do vampires never invite trolls to their dinner parties ?

They can't stand all that goblin !

★

What do sea monsters eat ?

Fish and ships !

★

What did the vampire do when someone accused him of drinking blood ?

He didn't bat an eyelid !

★

Why should you never invite monsters to a housewarming party ?

Because they bring flame throwers !

★

What do you give a monster that feels sick ?

Plenty of room !

Why should you never play cricket with Dracula?

Because he might let his vampire bat!

★

I see Dracula has a new job –
he's a cashier in a blood bank!

★

You know that a barking vampire dog never bites...
but when it stops barking, you'd better run!

How does a werewolf sign his letters ?

Best vicious !

★

What do you call a hairy monster that's lost ?

A where-am-I wolf !

★

What do you call an escaped hairy monster ?

A where's-he-gone wolf !

★

What is Frankenstein's worst nightmare ?

Being nude in a room full of people –
without a stitch on !

★

What do you get if you put a monster on your roof ?

A bite on the tiles !

When Dracula put on his coat one evening his wife asked if he was going out with his friends. "No, dear," he replied. "Just popping out for a bite!"

★

What is a ghost's car called ?

Squeals on wheels !

★

What is Dracula's favourite type of coffee ?

De - coffinated !

What does Dracula have fitted to the front of his car ?

Head vamps !

★

Which monster ate the three bears ?

Ghouldilocks !

★

What did Dracula say when someone said his teeth were ugly ?

I'll fang you not to say that !

★

What sort of view do you get from the top of a pyramid ?

As Pharaoh the eye can see !

★

What would you be if your daddy was a mummy and you were musical ?

A wrap singer !

What pets does Dracula own?

A blood hound and a ghoul fish!

★

Why do vampires have steady nerves?

Because they are as ghoul as cucumbers!

★

Why do zombies always look so tired?

They are dead on their feet!

Why did Dracula advertise for a housekeeper ?

He wanted some new blood in the house !

★

Did you hear about the monster who went into a restaurant and ordered crocodile and chips ?

He was in a hurry so he shouted, "and make it snappy !"

★

If you're good at writing, Dracula has a job for you...

...he's looking for someone to answer his fang mail,

...and to take on the job as his crypt writer !

★

How do you get a message to a deep sea monster ?

Drop him a line !

★

Why is the sea monster wet ?

Because the seaweed !

How do you know what a deep sea monster looks like ?

He's the one with the wavy hair !

★

How do you know if a monster fancies you ?

He'll roll his eyes at you !

And what should you do if that happens ?

Roll them back before someone steps on them !

★

In the monster version of Snow White, what are the seven dwarves called ?

Snacks !

Why do vampires avoid arguments ?

They hate to get cross !

★

What do monsters call a crowded swimming pool ?

Soup !

★

The monster went to his doctor and complained of a split personality.

Do sit down, the doctor said, and begin by telling me which one of you is paying !

★

"I think I need new glasses," said the short sighted monster.

"You certainly do," replied the dentist !

★

Who do you telephone to rent a Dracula costume ?

Vamp - hire !

How do you know if you had a drunken vampire at your party?

There are fang marks on the tomato sauce bottle!

★

What's yellow and green with red spots?

A monster with the measels!

★

What do you call a monster with a broken leg?

A hoblin!

Oh, red-eyed vampire in the night,
you nearly gave my heart a fright.
All black and shiny, glistening red,
from pongy toes to slithery head.
If you had hoped to drink my blood,
and hoped that it would do you good,
I think you made a big mistake,
'cos I'd just been out for a steak!

★

Why did Dracula want to keep his baby teeth for all eternity?

Because a fang of beauty is a joy forever!

Why did the vampire go to the blood donor centre ?

To get lunch !

★

What do baby sea monsters play with ?

Doll-fins !

★

Where do monsters sleep ?

Anywhere they want to !

★

Can you stick vampires to your window ?

Yes – they are suckers !

How do vampires start a duel ?

They stand Drac to Drac !

★

When do ghosts wear red jackets and ride horses ?

When they go out fox haunting !

★

Why are owls so brave at night ?

Because they don't give a hoot for ghosts, monsters or vampires !

What did the old vampire say when he broke his teeth ?

Fangs for the memories !

★

Why do vampires holiday at the seaside ?

They love to be near the ghostguard stations !

★

Why did the ghost go to the bicycle shop ?

He needed some new spooks for his front wheel !

★

What do you call a vampire who really likes dentists ?

An extractor fan !

What tops off a ghost's ice cream sundae?

Whipped scream!

★

Why do monsters like to stand in a ring?

They love being part of a vicious circle!

★

What do you call a ghostly teddy bear?

Winnie the OOOoooooOooooohhHHhhhhh!

What do you call a futuristic android who comes back in time to plant seeds ?

Germinator !

★

And what do you call his twin brother ?

Germinator II !

★

Why was the cannibal expelled from school ?

For buttering up the teacher !

★

What sort of wolf can you wear ?

A wear wolf !

★

What sort of wolf delivers Christmas presents ?

Santa Claws !

Why do ghosts catch cold so easily ?

They get chilled to the marrow !

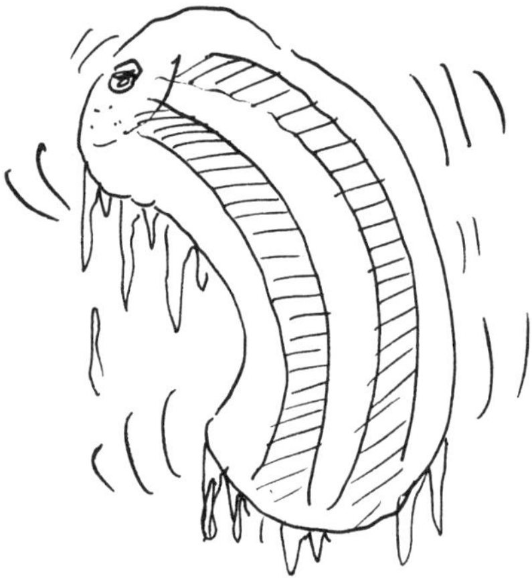

★

What do you call a lazy skeleton ?

Bone idle !

★

Why didn't the vampire laugh at the joke
about the wooden stake ?

He didn't get the point !

What do you call a scary, bony creature that staggers around making strange wailing noises ?

A supermodel making a record !

★

Why are skeletons no good at telling lies ?

Because you can see right through them !

★

What should you say when a vampire gives you a present ?

Fang you very much !

What does a vampire fear the most ?

Tooth decay !

★

What do monsters like to pour on their Sunday dinner ?

Grave-y !

★

What do you call a ghostly haircut with long curly strands of hair ?

Deadlocks !

★

What do ghosts like with their food ?

A little whine !

What do you get if you cross the abominable snowman and Count Dracula?

Severe frostbite!

★

Where is the invisible man?

No idea, I haven't seen him around for ages!

★

Where do vampires like to go for their holidays?

The Dead Sea!

★

Why did the two vampire bats get married?

Because they were heels over heads in love!

What do you get if you shoot a
werewolf with a silver bullet ?

A very interesting rug !

★

Did you hear about the monster who
fell asleep in an empty coffin ?

It was a grave mistake !

★

What sort of jobs do spooks like ?

Dead end jobs !

★

Did you hear about the vampire burglar who
was caught red handed ?

They caught him fang to rights !

★

What do you call a stupid vampire ?

A clot !

What did the pirate get when he smashed a skeleton up in a fight ?

A skull and very cross bones !

★

Where do skeletons cook their meals ?

In a skullery !

★

What do you call a young skeleton in a cap and uniform ?

A skullboy !

What is a monster's favourite play?

Romeo and Ghouliet!

★

Why are vampires so thin?

They eat necks to nothing!

★

Why are hyenas always falling out?

They always have a bone to pick with each other!

★

Who delivers Christmas presents to vampires?

Sack-ula!

What vampire can you wear to protect
you from the rain ?

Mac - ula !

★

What is the fairy tale about a girl who
falls in love with a really ugly loaf of bread ?

Beauty and the yeast !

★

When they got married, what sort of children
did they have ?

Bun-shees !

★

Why did Goldilocks go to Egypt ?

She wanted to see the mummy bear !

AND, SPEAKING OF MUMMIES...

Mummy, mummy, what is a vampire ?

Be quiet and eat your soup before it clots !

★

Mummy, mummy, what is a werewolf ?

Be quiet and comb your face !

★

Mummy, mummy, I don't like my uncle Fred !

Well, just leave him on the side of your plate and eat the rest !

★

Mummy, mummy, I'm just going out for a quick bite to eat !

OK, but make sure you're back in your coffin before daybreak !

What do you get if you cross Dracula with Al Capone!

A fangster!

★

What did the monster say when the vampire asked for his daughter's hand in marriage?

OK, we'll eat the rest!

★

What lies at the bottom of the sea and shivers?

A nervous wreck!

★

Why can you never get through to a vampire bat on the telephone?

Because they always hang up!

★

Why didn't the spook win the lottery?

He didn't have a ghost of a chance!

What should you wear when you go out for a drink with a vampire ?

A metal collar !

★

What do you call a young woman who hunts vampires ?

A Miss Stake !

★

What do the police call it when they watch a vampire's house ?

A stake out !

Why did the vampire put tomato sauce on his sandwiches?

He was a vegetarian!

★

What did the ghostly show jumper always score?

A clear round!

★

What did the young ghost call his mum and dad?

His trans-parents!

★

Why don't you have to worry what you say to the werewolf computer engineer?

His bark is worse than his byte!

What sort of jokes do werewolves like best ?

Howlers !

★

What happens when a werewolf meets a vampire ?

He doesn't turn a hair !

★

Why wasn't the werewolf allowed to get off the lunar spaceship ?

Because the moon was full !

★

Why did the werewolf start going to the gym ?

Because he liked the changing rooms !

What did the train driver say to the werewolf ?

Keep the change !

★

Why did the werewolf steal underwear
when the moon was full ?

Because his doctor told him a change
was as good as a vest !

★

What sort of news do werewolves fear ?

Silver bulletins !

Why did the shy werewolf hide in a cupboard every full moon ?

Because he didn't like anyone to see him changing !

★

How do you grow a werewolf from a seed ?

Just use plenty of fur-tiliser !

★

How do mummies knock on doors ?

They wrap as hard as they can !

★

Why was the mummy done up in brightly coloured sparkly paper ?

He was gift-wrapped !

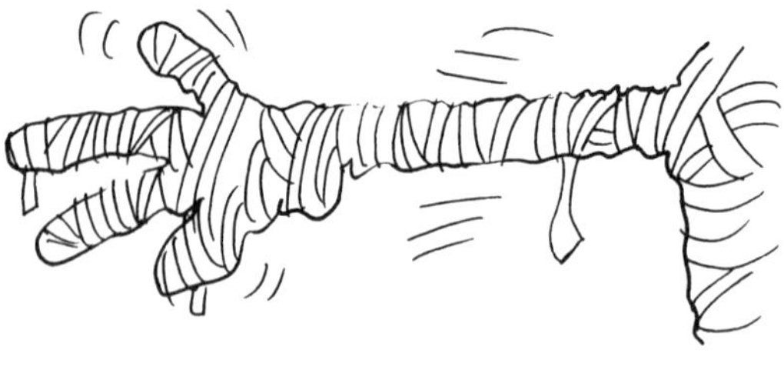

What does it say on the entrance to a mummy's home?

Toot and come in!

★

What pop group did the young mummies join?

A boy bandage!

★

What do children in Egypt call their parents?

Mummy and daddy of course!

Why was the Egyptian prince worried ?

Because his mummy and daddy were both mummies !

★

What do mummies shout when they are on a sinking boat ?

A bandage ship !

★

What do mummies do to relax ?

They just unwind a little !

★

Why was the mummy's leg stiff ?

Because someone had been winding him up !

What are the scariest dinosaurs ?

Terror - dactyls !

★

Why are mummies good at keeping secrets ?

They can keep things under wraps for centuries !

★

What did the monster say when it saw someone going past on a mountain bike ?

"Ah! Meals on wheels !"

★

What did the ghost of the owl say ?

"Too-wit too-woooooooooooo..."

Why did the vampire like eating chewy sweets ?

He liked something to get his teeth into !

★

Who was the winner of the headless horse race ?

No-one, they all finished neck and neck !

★

What did the President of the USA say to the giant ape when he won the lottery ?

Kong - ratulations !

DUMB AND DUMBER

What did the parakeet say when he finished shopping ?

Just put it on my bill !

★

Did you hear about Big Chief Running Water ?

He had two sons, so he called them Hot and Cold !

★

How do you confuse an idiot ?

I'll tell you tomorrow !

★

What does Tarzan eat on Saturday nights ?

Fish and chimps !

★

Did you hear about the idiot who went to a car boot sale ?

He now owns six car boots !

How did the midget alien get into the police force ?

He lied about his age !

★

What is yellow and highly dangerous ?

Shark-infested custard !

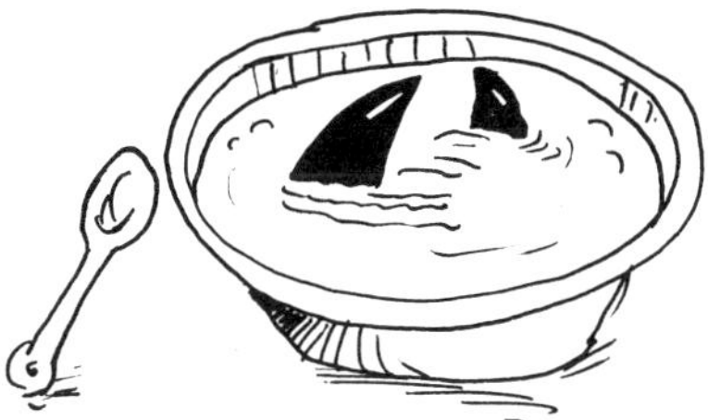

★

Why should you dial carefully if you phone Mr Wing in China ?

You might ring the Wong number !

★

Why did the orange stop rolling down the hill?

It ran out of juice !

What did they award the man who invented the door knocker ?

The No-bell Prize !

★

What happens when a witch catches the flu ?

Everyone gets a cold spell !

★

Where did the stonemason take his girlfriend ?

To a rock concert !

★

Did you hear where the fizzy drinks maker took his girlfriend ?

To a pop concert !

★

What does an idiot do when he wins the *Round the World Yacht Race* ?

He does a lap of honour !

What happened when the idiot made

Someone hijacked it!

★

Did you hear about the robbers who fell in the sea?

They started a crime wave!

★

Why did the idiot apply for a job as a language teacher?

Because someone told him he spoke perfect rubbish!

★

Waiter, can I have my lunch on the patio?

Certainly, Sir, but most people find a plate more sensible!

What do you call a Roman emperor with flu ?

Julius Sneezer !

★

Why was the trout's piano off key ?

Because he couldn't find the piano tuna !

★

I bought myself a pocket calculator for Christmas - now I know exactly how many pockets I have !

★

What has six legs and flies ?

A witch giving her cat a ride !

What is bright orange and sounds like a parrot ?

A carrot !

★

Did you hear about the failed magician ?

He had one half brother and one half sister !

★

Mmmmm ! This jam sponge cake is
lovely and warm !

It should be, the cat's been sitting on
it all afternoon !

★

Why did the robot need a manicure ?

He had rusty nails !

★

What did the werewolf say to the vampire ?

It's been so nice getting to gnaw you !

What do you get if you cross a space suit and a saddle?

A horse - tranaut!

★

What is the best thing to do when a hippo sneezes?

Get out of the way!

★

Doctor, Doctor, I keep thinking I'm a goat!

And how long has this been going on?

Oh, ever since I was a kid!

★

How do you spell 'mousetrap' in three letters!

C – A – T!

★

What is red and cheeky?

Tomato sauce!

First cannibal - What are you cooking for dinner ?

Second cannibal - Shut up and get back in the oven !

★

Our tyres are the best that money can buy - we skid you not !

★

What's thick and black and comes out of the ground and shouts 'knickers!' ?

Crude oil !

★

What's thick and black and comes out of the ground and shouts 'underwear!' ?

Refined oil !

★

Which age did the mummies live in ?

The band - age !

I love all my teachers,
from my head down to my belly.
I love to do my homework,
even though I miss the telly.
I love to do detention,
and I love to work real late.
I polish all the teachers' shoes,
I really think they're great.
They're kind and smart and helpful,
they're delicate and gentle.
And I am - yes, you've guessed it -
- very, very mental !

★

How does a male octopus ask a female octopus to marry him ?

Can I have your hand, your hand, your hand, your hand... !

★

When the monster had finished eating his human, he threw the wristwatch onto a pile in the corner.

His friend asked him why he did this.

He said, "It's too time-consuming !"

A Yeti who came from Basmati,
Woke up one day feeling quite hearty.
It's those climbers I ate,
He said as he licked the plate.
I can't wait for the rescue party!

★

Did you hear about the bird that lived underground?

He was a mynah bird!

★

What do you get if you cross a vampire with a petrol pump?

Something that makes a hole in your car and sucks out all the petrol!

What does a witch take on holiday ?

Her sleeping hag !

★

Where does Dracula go in the summer ?

To a holiday vamp !

★

What was the Chinese air force commander called ?

The Wing Commander !

★

What did the doctor say to the invisible man after he had swallowed some coins ?

I can't see any change in you !

★

Why was Cinderella so bad at football ?

She had a pumpkin for a coach !

Why do witches go to hot countries ?

For a spell in the sun !

★

My uncle came in white as a sheet. He said, "I've just seen a ghost. Make me a stiff drink."

So I put some starch in his coffee !

★

What insect do you find before the sea ?

The B !

★

There were two eggs in a frying pan at a monastery. One said to the other, "Any minute now it's going to be out of the frying pan into the friar."

★

Did you hear about the cowboy whose dog fell over a cliff ?

He said, "Dawg gone !"

Why couldn't the butterfly go to the dance ?

It was a moth ball !

★

What do you get if you cross a canary with a monster ?

A broken cage !

★

Why are vampires so stupid ?

Because blood is thicker than water !

Why can you never trick a snake monster ?

Because you can't pull his leg !

★

What do you get if you cross a bird with a snake ?

A feather boa constrictor !

★

Did you hear about the sculptor's son ?

He was a chip off the old block !

★

What's the difference between margarine and a goat ?

You mean you can't tell margarine from a butter ?

★

Did you hear about the idiot who sold his television to raise the money to buy a remote control for it ?

Or his brother, who sold his personal stereo to get the money to buy batteries for it ?

Why did you decide to become a cat burglar ?

My doctor told me to take things quietly !

★

Why do flamingos lift one leg ?

Because if they lifted both legs they would fall over !

★

What was the first thing that Henry VIII did on coming to the throne ?

He sat down !

★

How many sheep does it take to make a sweater ?

Wow - I didn't even know sheep could knit !

★

How do you make gold soup ?

Put 14 carrots in it !

Operator, get me the king of the jungle!

I'm sorry but the lion is busy right now!

★

What's the difference between a crazy rabbit and a forged bank note?

One is a mad bunny, the other is bad money!

★

What happened when the monsters ate the comedian?

It was a feast of fun!

★

Waiter - this lemonade is cloudy!

No it isn't Sir, it's the glass that's dirty!

★

Where were all the Kings of Italy crowned?

On the head!

Did you hear about the triangle player who disappeared from the orchestra...

...while they were playing the Bermuda waltz ?

★

Did you hear about the librarian who got carried away...

...while he was reading The Invasion Of The Body Snatchers ?

★

Waiter, waiter, there's a fly in my soup !

Sorry Madam, I didn't know you were vegetarian !

I'm never going to follow in my father's footsteps,
I faint at the sight of blood!

Was your father a doctor?

No, a vampire!

★

What do you think the invention of the safety match had on society?

I'd say it was a striking achievement!

★

Why is a lazy schoolboy the exact opposite of Robinson Crusoe?

Because Robinson Crusoe got all his work done by Friday!

★

Did you hear about the dog who went to a flea circus?

No, what happened?

He stole the show!

Doctor, last week I went glass blowing and instead of blowing out I breathed in.

Don't tell me, you've got a pane in your stomach!

★

Three badly made robots were playing cards...

One threw his hand in...

Another rolled his eyes... across the floor...

The third one laughed his head off!

★

A really bad jazz band had just finished a song.

"Any requests?" they called to the audience.

"Do you know 'San Francisco'?" replied one member of the audience.

"Yes, of course," replied the band leader.

"Please go there and play!"

Why did the car driver close his eyes ?

Because the traffic light was changing !

★

Why did the witches mail rattle ?

It was a chain letter !

★

Why do vampires dislike pointed stakes ?

Because they know that it's rude to point !

What do you call a man who can complete any job in 30 seconds?

Arthur Minute!

★

What happened when two wasps had a fight?

There was a terrible buzzt-up!

★

Name seven things that are grey, four-legged and have a trunk!

Six elephants and a mouse going on holiday!

★

Why did the elephant cover his trunk in suncream?

Because he didn't want to get it sunburned!

★

How does a witch-bride get to the altar?

On a groom stick!

What's big, green, and ugly and never smiles ?

The Incredible Sulk !

★

Did you hear about the ghost who works at police headquarters ?

He's the Chief In-spectre !

★

How do you know if an elephant has been in the fridge ?

You'll find its footprints in the butter !

★

How do you make a Mexican chilli ?

Take him to the North Pole !

★

Doctor - Is your cough better now ?

Patient - Oh yes much better. I've been practising for weeks !

Two idiots were fishing in a lake and were catching lots of fish.

They decided to come back the following weekend and catch even more fish, but they were concerned that they would not be able to find the exact spot on the lake when they next came.

Then one of them had a brilliant idea - he painted a red X on the side of the boat !

★

Why should you never fall asleep on a train ?

Because they run over sleepers !

★

What sort of cereal do snowmen eat ?

Snowflakes !

YOU KNOW IT'S A BAD SIGN WHEN...

...you see weathermen eating beans !

...travel agents close their shops and go on holiday !

...psychiatrists keep changing their minds !

...there's a fight in the chip shop, and people get battered !

...people call in a sturgeon when they get a fish bone stuck in their throat !

...a schoolboy gets locked in a cage in the classroom because he is teacher's pet !

...a maths teacher smiles !

...the plumber brings a plug for your new bath, because he thinks it is electric !

★

Butler – Sir, there's a ghost outside in the corridor. What shall I do ?

Master – Tell him I can't see him !

How do bees get to school ?

On the school buzz !

★

How do you know when your school bus is old ?

When the seats are covered in mammoth hide !

★

What do you get if you cross a science room and a dog ?

A lab !

★

What do you call a cake you eat in the bath ?

A sponge !

★

Remember that before you give someone a piece of your mind, you should always check that you will have enough left over for yourself !

If I should win the lottery,

Think how much fun my life would be.

No more school, or work at home,

No more school dinners that taste like foam.

No more lines, no more pain,

Just lots of telly and sweets and games !

★

Why should you always be thankful to pigs ?

Because you should never take them for grunted !

★

Why do swimming teachers like elephants ?

Because they never forget their trunks !

★

Did you hear about the elephant who sued the airline ?

His trunk got caught in the X-ray machine !

Did you hear about the vampire who
swallowed a sheep ?

He said he felt baaaad !

★

How do you cut water ?

With a sea-saw !

★

Did you hear about the prisoner
who talked very slowly ?

It took him 25 years to finish his sentence !

★

Did you hear about the sick clock ?

It was run down !

★

Did you hear about the vampire who
loved ballroom dancing ?

He especially liked the vaultz !

A man decided to start a chicken farm and bought 24 chicks to get started.

A week later he bought another 24 and then another 24 the week after that.

When his friend asked how his chicken farm was coming along the man replied, "Not one of them has grown yet. I wonder if I'm planting them too deep ?"

★

What time do you always go to the dentist ?

Tooth-hurty !

How do you make a Swiss roll ?

Push him down an Alp !

★

What happens when you feed gunpowder to chickens ?

You get an eggsplosion !

★

What does a caterpillar do on January 1st?

He turns over a new leaf !

★

Teacher - I'll teach you to be clever in my class !

Pupil - At last, a lesson I'll be interested in!

★

Why did the deaf Italian waiter smear pasta sauce on people's ankles ?

Because he thought they asked for spaghetti below-the-knees !

What do you get from a nudist pig ?

Streaky bacon !

★

What did Fred Flintstone shout when he had a cold ?

Yabba - Dabba - Atish - ooo !

★

Why did the human cannon ball consider himself a failure ?

Because he was always being fired !

★

What is the difference between electricity and lightning ?

Lightning is free !

My friend John believes in free speech...which is why he comes round to my house to telephone people !

★

What is a forum ?

A two - um plus a two - um !

★

The new doctor is so witty - he'll have you in stitches !

I hope not - I've only come to see him about my sore throat !

★

Catacomb - a hair cleaning device for cats !

★

A load of bees were getting very hot and bothered one summer's day. The queen bee asked what the trouble was...

"Swarm," came the reply !

Did the doctor give you anything for your wind ?

Yes, he gave me this kite !

★

Why did the doctor write on your foot ?

He said it was a footnote !

★

Which Shakespeare play is about pigs ?

Hamlet !

★

Johnny, I despair of your spelling mistakes and poor punctuation. Where is your grammar ?

She's at home watching the telly, Miss!

What sort of animal do you need when it's cold ?

An otter !

★

How do you cure a headache ?

Put your head through a window and the pane will disappear !

★

A bird in the hand...is likely to poo on your wrist !

★

Where do space monks live ?

In a moon - astry !

Where do they keep old cows ?

In a moooseum !

★

What do you do if you swallow a wristwatch ?

Take a laxative to help pass the time !

★

Why did the lemon refuse to fight the orange ?

Because it was yellow !

★

What is always dressing ?

Mayonnaise !

★

Knock, Knock
Who's there ?
Howard.
Howard who ?
Howard I know ?

What do you give a pig with a sore snout ?

Oinkment !

★

Teacher – In the olden days, false teeth were made of wood. Do you know what tree the wood came from ?

Pupil – The gum tree ?

★

What did the careful robot say ?

Look before you bleep !

★

Teacher - Wilson, what is a telescope ?

Wilson - Something that you can watch TV with from a long way off ?

★

Why are dinosaurs extinct ?

Because male and female dinosaurs refused to get evolved with each other !

Why was the ghost's son asked to leave the school ?

Because he was clearly too high spirited !

★

When's the best time to buy a budgerigar ?

When they're going cheep !

★

Why was the genie in the lamp angry ?

Someone rubbed him up the wrong way !

★

Why do football teams have to practise so much when they play against zombies ?

Because they face stiff competition !

★

Boy cannibal to mother cannibal – Mummy, mummy, can I bring my friend over for tea ?

Mother cannibal – Of course, dear, put him in the fridge and we'll have him later !

How do you make anti-freeze ?

Send her to the North Pole !

★

Johnson, what are you doing standing out there in the rain ?

Getting wet, Sir !

★

Why are elephants so wrinkled ?

Have you ever tried ironing one ?

Did you drink your medicine
after your bath ?

No, after I drank the bath I couldn't
manage the medicine !

★

What do you call a pimple on a Tyrannosaurus Rex ?

A dino-sore !

★

Our parrot lays star-shaped eggs !

Wow - does it talk as well ?

It just says the one word - "OUCH !"

★

Grandad, do you know how to
impersonate a frog ?

I think so, young Eric, but why ?

Because Mum says that when you
croak we'll be rich !

Doctor, my hair keeps falling out - can you give me something to keep it in ?

Yes, here's a paper bag !

★

How does a vampire start a letter ?

'Tomb it may concern...'

★

What did the inscription outside the pyramid say ?

Satisfaction guaranteed - or your mummy back !

★

Which city is the most shocking ?

Electri - city !

★

What fish would you find on a battery-powered shoe ?

An electric heel !

YOBS AND GIRLS

My brother is the school swot !

Does he do well in exams ?

No - he just kills flies !

★

My uncle keeps a pig under his bed.

What about the smell ?

It's ok - the pig doesn't mind it !

★

My sister was engaged to a man with a wooden leg.

Did she marry him ?

No, she broke it off !

★

My wife said that if I didn't give up playing golf she would divorce me !

Wow - that must have been a tough decision to make !

Yes - and I really miss her now !

My boyfriend is called Fog !

Is that because he is wisp-like and mysterious ?

No, it's because he's wet, grey and thick !

★

Headteacher - That is the stupidest girl in the whole school !

Parent - That's my daughter you're talking about !

Headteacher - Oh, I'm terribly sorry !

Parent - You're sorry - how do you think I feel ?

★

Our drama teacher says I've got the perfect face for radio !

My English teacher says my handwriting is
so bad I could be a doctor !

★

My science teacher says I could be an astronaut...
because I have nothing but space between my ears !

★

Now, children, what were you before you
started school ?

"Happy !"

★

My girlfriend tried on a mud pack, and it really made
her look better... until she washed it off !

★

Wow! You look like a million dollars !

Do you really think so ?

Yes, you're all green and wrinkly !

Have you heard about the magic tractor ?

It turned into a field !

★

What do you call a fly with no wings ?

A walk !

★

What sort of animal is best at getting up in the morning ?

A llama clock !

The teacher asked the class to write an essay about what they would do if they won the lottery!

Wilkinson handed in a blank sheet of paper.

"What is the meaning of this?" she asked.

"It's what I'd do if I won the lottery - nothing!"

★

Melissa was playing the flute - very badly!

Her brother said, "You should be on the television playing that!"

"Wow, do you think I'm good enough?" she replied.

"No, but at least I could turn you off!"

Why did the school idiot buy a seahorse ?

Because he wanted to play water polo !

★

Piano teacher – Your fingers are absolutely filthy!

Pupil – It's ok Miss, I'm only playing the black keys !

★

What happened to the cat that ate a ball of wool ?

It gave birth to mittens !

★

My little Geoff is a wonder child...the teachers at his school often wonder if he'll ever learn anything !

★

What do you make with a giant deck of playing cards ?

A big deal !

Why did the crocodile buy his son a camera ?

Because he was always snapping !

★

What would you do if a jellyfish stung you ?

I'd break every bone in its body !

★

I was about to fight the school bully when my sister threw rotten eggs at me.

What did she do that for ?

She said that I was egging him on !

Ants have got amazing brains. Have you noticed how they always know when you're having a picnic?

★

I've just seen a black cat!

That's good, black cats are lucky!

This one is, it's eaten your lunch!

★

Mother - Doctor, my little girl's swallowed my pen.

Doctor - Don't worry you can borrow mine!

★

What did the fat man say when he sat down at the dinner table?

"Just think - all this food is going to waist!"

★

Why did Belinda give cough medicine to the pony?

Because Sally told her it was a little horse!

Please sir, I wouldn't get into trouble for something I haven't done would I ?

Of course not, Richards, that would be unfair !

I'm glad you said that - I haven't done my homework !

★

If God could make a woman out of a man's rib - what did he do with all the leftovers ?

★

My sewing teacher was away from school ill. When I asked how she was feeling she said "Sew, sew !"

★

What did the clockmaker say when he was burgled ?

He's taken my valuable time !

★

What sort of books do dwarves read ?

Collections of short stories !

What would you find in a rabbit's library?

Bucks!

★

What do you get if you cross a brain surgeon and a herd of cows?

A cow-operation!

★

What did the overweight ballet dancer perform?

The dance of the sugar plump fairy!

Why do monsters have to pay twice when they go to the zoo ?

Once to get in and once to get out !

★

Of course your shoes hurt – you've put them on the wrong feet !

But they're the only feet I have !

★

What did one salt pot maker say to the other salt pot maker when they first met ?

Shake !

★

What did the alien say to the petrol pump ?

"Take your finger out of your ear when I'm talking to you !"

★

What's bright red, runs on petrol and eats corn flakes ?

A motor cycle – I lied about the corn flakes !

I just love eating burgers, but they make my belly so fat !

Have you tried to diet ?

No - what colour would be best ?

★

Doctor, doctor, my sister thinks she's a lift !

You had better tell her to come in and see me !

I can't - she doesn't stop at this floor !

★

I met my first girlfriend at a printmaker's disco...but it didn't last, she wasn't the right type for me !

What work does Mrs Claus give Santa Claus
to do in the garden ?

Ho Ho Hoeing !

★

Why did the schoolboy bite the dentist ?

Because he got on his nerves !

★

If I were a schoolboy,
all over again,
I'd work really hard,
and never get the cane.
I'd pass exams,
just like that,
I'd even remember,
to wear my cap.
Then one day,
if my dream came true,
I'd be a teacher,
just like you !
I hope you like my poem,
I don't want to make you sad, but...
it was written by a boy,
who is totally MAD !

Why is it easy to swindle a sheep ?

Because it is so easy to pull the wool over its eyes !

★

What do elves eat at parties ?

Fairy cakes !

★

Where do fish like going for their holidays ?

Finland !

★

Why did the carpenter go to the doctor ?

He had a saw hand !

How do you help Frankenstein's monster ?

Give him a hand when he needs it !

★

How should you show your appreciation to a vampire ?

With a fang-you letter !

★

This homework looks a though it has been written by your father ?

Well it will do, I borrowed his pen !

What do you call two witched living together?

Broom mates!

★

What were Tarzan's last words?

"Who moved that viiiine!"

★

What did they call the cowboy after someone stole all his cash?

Skint Eastwood!

★

An apple a day keeps the doctor away...

An onion a day keeps everyone else away!

★

How did the schoolboy stop the elephant from smelling?

He tied a knot in its trunk!

Arnold, you are good at picking up music – go and move the piano from the music room to the assembly hall !

★

What's cleverer than a talking cat ?

A spelling bee !

★

What is a maybe ?

A bee born in May !

★

Jenson, I think you need glasses !

But I'm already wearing glasses !

In that case I need glasses !

★

How do you wake chickens in the morning ?

With an alarm cluck !

What do computer operators eat for lunch?

Chips!

★

How do you stop a head cold going to your chest?

Easy - tie a knot in your neck!

★

Why shouldn't you try to swim on a full stomach?

Because it's easier to swim on a full swimming pool!

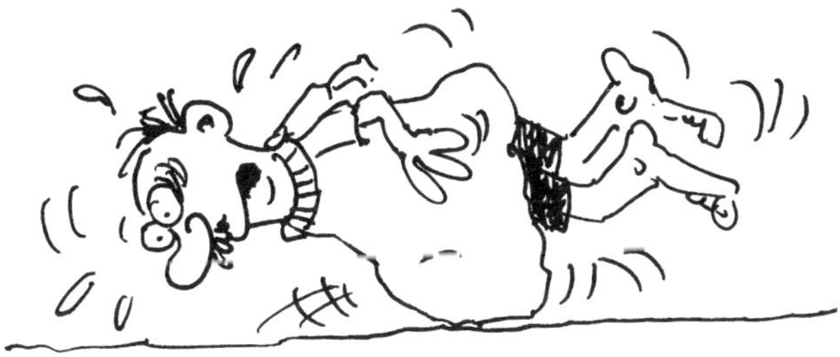

★

When is a car not a car?

When it turns into a garage!

Which famous knight never won a single battle ?

Sir Endor !

★

Hear about the famous inventors who failed to invent the aeroplane ?

They were the Wrong Brothers !

★

What happened to the Scottish schoolboy who washed his kilt ?

Now he can't do a fling with it !

★

Why did the sword-swallower swallow an umbrella ?

He wanted to put something away for a rainy day !

★

What do you call a man with soil on his head ?

Pete !

How do you know if your little brother is turning into a fridge?

See if a little light comes on whenever he opens his mouth!

★

What is the coldest part of the North Pole?

An explorer's nose!

★

Why is that man standing in the sink?

He's a tap dancer!

What do you call a man with a tree growing out of his head?

Ed - Wood!

★

Where do rabbits learn to fly?

In the Hare Force!

★

How did the witch know she was getting better?

Because the doctor let her get out of bed for a spell!

What did the witch call her baby daughter ?

Wanda !

★

How do witch children listen to stories ?

Spellbound !

★

Why couldn't the elephants both go swimming at the same time ?

They only had one pair of trunks between them !

How do you make a baby snake cry ?'

Take away his rattle !

★

Why was the boy who had cake feeling upset ?

Because it was stomach cake !

★

Why was Cinderella rubbish at Games ?

Because she kept running away from the ball !

★

What were the 16 schoolboys playing in the telephone box ?

Squash !

★

Have you ever seen a man-eating tiger ?

No, but in the café next door I once saw a man eating chicken! !

What is the only true cure for dandruff ?

Baldness !

★

What should you buy if your hair falls out ?

A good vacuum cleaner !

★

A man went to see his doctor with a brick buried in his head. What was he suffering from ?

Falling arches !

Why was the boy staring at the orange juice ?

Because it said 'concentrate' !

★

Nurse – why are you putting Mr Smith's left leg in plaster? It's his right leg that's broken !

It's OK, I'm new so I'm practising on the left one first to make sure I do it properly!

★

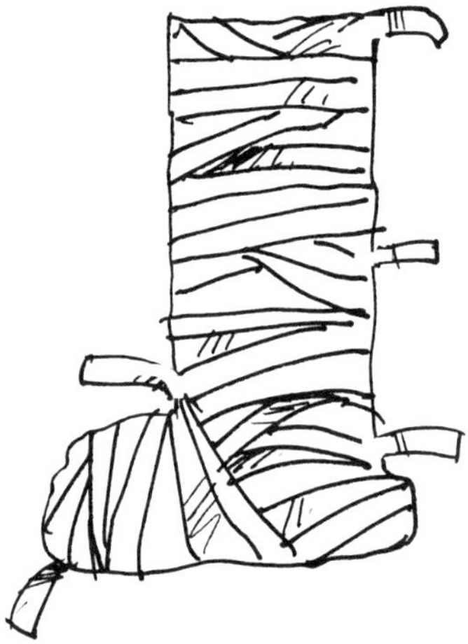

What sort of fish would you find in a bird cage ?

A perch !

★

What sort of fish would you find in a shoe ?

An eel !

What sort of dance do fish do at parties?

The conga!

★

Did you hear about the dog who was arrested?

He didn't pay a barking ticket!

★

Did you hear about the bungee jumper who shot up and down for 3 hours before they could bring him under control?

He had a yo-yo in his pocket!

What do you call the teacher in the school who gives out forms that you have to fill in ?

The form teacher !

★

Where did the rich cat live ?

In a mews cottage !

★

That girl over there thinks she's a tonsil !

But she's very nicely dressed...

Yes, she thinks the doctor is taking her out tonight !

What has a bottom at the top?

Your legs!

★

Why was the butcher worried?

His job was at steak!

★

What position did the pile of wood play in the soccer team?

De-fence!

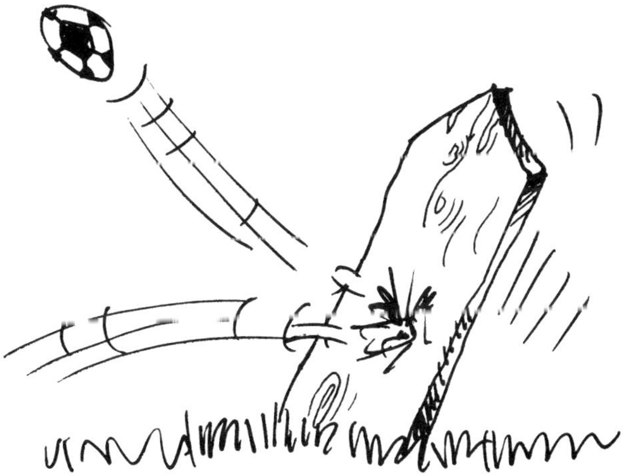

Why couldn't the slow boxer get a drink at the party?

Because everyone beat him to the punch!

★

Why did the French farmer only keep the one chicken?

Because in France one egg is un oeuf!

★

What did the farmer say when all his cows charged him at once?

I'm on the horns of a dilemma here!

What do you call two spiders who are just married?

Newlywebs!

★

What sort of ring is always square?

A boxing ring!

★

What sort of snake will tell on you?

A grass snake!

★

What sort of queue is always straight?

A snooker cue!

What sort of animals make the best TV presenters?

Gnus - readers!

★

POINTLESS INVENTIONS...

Camouflage for stick insects!

Disposable rubbish bags!

Colour radio!

Invisible traffic lights!

Plastic tea bags!

Waterproof soap!

Fireproof petrol!

Why do golfers carry a spare sock ?

Because they might get a hole in one !

★

What did the driver say when he ran over a biscuit ?

Crumbs !

★

What is white when it's dirty and
black when it's clean ?

A blackboard !

★

What did one eye say to the other eye ?

Between you and me something smells !

★

What do you call a deer with no eyes ?

No idea !

What do ghosts eat in Italian restaurants ?

Spook - ghetti !

★

Which two letters are bad for your teeth ?

DK !

★

Teacher - You missed school yesterday, didn't you ?

Pupil - Not very much !

★

Did you hear about the posh chef with an attitude problem ?

He had a chip on his shoulder !

How do monkeys make toast ?

They put some bread under a gorilla !

★

I once met a man from Hong Kong,
who'd been jogging for twenty years long.
He was terribly sweaty,
he looked like a yeti,
and his feet had a terrible pong !

★

What sort of footwear do bananas make ?

Slippers !

I hear you've just invented gunpowder ?

Yes, I was using some candles to light my laboratory and it came to me in a flash !

★

Why did the doctor take his nose to pieces ?

He wanted to see what made it run !

★

Why is it dangerous to tell jokes to Humpty Dumpty ?

He might crack up !

Why do pens get sent to prison?

To do long sentences!

★

What was the parrot doing in prison?

It was a jail-bird!

★

What is the name of the detective who sings quietly to himself while solving crimes?

Sherlock Hums!

Why did the farmer feed his pigs
on sugar and vinegar ?

He wanted some sweet and sour pork !

★

What do you call
a Scottish
dentist ?

Phil McCavity !

★

Why is the soil
in my garden
always dry ?

Because you
have leeks !

★

What did the little boy say when he
wanted his big brother to give
him back his building bricks ?

Lego !

What do you get if you cross a
parrot and a spider ?

A walkie-talkie !

★

What happened to the man who
stole a lorry load of eggs ?

He gave himself up – he said he only did it for a yolk !

★

What kind of rose has a bark ?

A dog rose !

★

Which is faster, hot or cold ?

Hot, because you can catch a cold !

★

How do you start a jelly baby race ?

Ready – set – go !

What sort of music was invented by fish ?

Sole music !

★

What do rabbits use to keep their hair in place ?

Hare-spray !

★

What gets smaller the more you put in it ?

A hole in the ground !

Waiter, why is there a dead fly in my soup ?

Well, you surely don't expect to get a live one at these prices !

★

Stop ! This is a one-way street !

Well, I'm only going one way !

Yes, but everyone else is going the other way !

Well, you're a policeman, make them turn round !

★

Mary had a little lamb,
which she dressed in pretty blouses,
she also had a ferret,
which she put down naughty boys' trousers !

★

Why do cows have horns ?

Because they would look pretty silly with bells on their heads !

What is the thing that is most read at Christmas ?

Rudolph's nose !

★

Why do toolmakers always escape from fires ?

They know the drill !

★

What did the stupid burglar do when he saw a 'WANTED' poster outside the police station ?

He went in and applied for the job !

★

What self defence method do mice use ?

Ka - rat - e !

Son – I can't go to school today, I don't feel well.

Mother – Where don't you feel well ?

Son – In school !

★

What's green and round and goes up and down ?

A pea in a lift !

★

What goes MOOOOOZ ?

A jet flying backwards !

★

Did you hear about the pilot who bailed out ?

He said, "Bi-plane" !

★

Mum, I'm feeling sick as a dog

Hang on while I call the vet !

Thirty people were sheltering under an umbrella. How many of them got wet ?

None - it wasn't raining !

★

Why are burglars such good tennis players ?

Because they spend such a lot of their time in courts !

If having hairy palms is the first sign of turning into a monster, what is the second ?

Looking for them !

★

Is that a new perfume I smell ?

It is, and you do !

★

What was on the haunted aeroplane ?

An air ghostess and a lot of high spirits !

★

Why did the witch take her small book of magic on holiday ?

The doctor told her to get away for a little spell !

★

What would you get if you combined a monster, a vampire, a werewolf and a ghost?

As far away as possible !

What do vampires use to phone their relatives ?

A terror - phone !

★

What are wasps' favourite flowers ?

Bee - gonias !

★

Why did the fly fly ?

Because the spider spied her !

What sort of monster is musical?

The one with A Flat head!

★

Why did the Romans build straight roads?

They didn't want anyone hiding round corners!

★

Where do Chinese vampires live?

Fang - Hai!

What do you call a dinosaur that keeps you awake at night ?

Bronto - snore - us !

★

Why do sea creatures go to so many parties ?

They like to have a whale of a time !

★

What is the name of the Australian dog drummer ?

Dingo Starr !

SICKLY AND MOROSE

Doctor - Put your tongue out and say Aaaah, please !

Patient - Aaaaah !

Doctor - Yuck ! You're not going to put that thing back in your mouth are you ?

★

WAITER, WAITER...

Hop into the kitchen and get me some frogs' legs !

Fetch me a crocodile sandwich, and make it snappy !

Get me the 24-hour special, and don't be all day about it !

★

Which vegetable can count the highest ?

A pot 8 - 0 !

★

What does the cannibal plastic surgeon charge ?

An arm and a leg !

Who is that at the door ?

A man with a wooden leg called Smith !

Really ? What is his other leg called ?

★

Who's that at the door ?

A man with one leg !

Tell him to hop it !

★

How can you mend King Kong's arm if he's twisted it ?

With a monkey wrench !

★

What dog loves to take bubble baths ?

A shampoodle !

Waiter, why is this dead mouse in my soup ?

I'm terribly sorry Sir, it should be in the pudding !

★

Why do aliens eat cabbage and sprouts ?

It puts colour in their cheeks !

★

How do bees qualify to make honey ?

They have to pass their hiving test !

★

What do you call a baby budgie ?

A budget !

What do you call pigs who write to each other ?

Pen friends !

★

Excuse me, how long will the next taxi be ?

About 2.3 metres !

★

What did the dog say when his owner stopped him chewing the newspaper ?

You took the words right out of my mouth !

★

What is the definition of dieting ?

Mind over fatter !

★

I thought you said he was a vet – he knows nothing about animal medicine at all !

I didn't say he was a vet – I said he had a sore throat – he's a hoarse doctor !

What sort of people make the best ghosts ?

The ones who are faint hearted !

★

Did you hear about the monster who carried on the family traditions ?

He was swallowing in his father's footsteps !

★

Why did the man send his alphabet soup back ?

Because he couldn't find words to describe it !

Why do chickens listen to the radio ?

It's their only form of hentertainment !

★

What sort of teeth can sing in a high voice ?

Falsettos !

★

What sort of music can you listen to in bed ?

Sheet music !

★

How do fleas train for the circus ?

They have to start from scratch !

★

What is the only thing that you can lose, and yet still have ?

Your temper !

Why do surgeons wear masks?

So that no-one will know who it was if they make a mistake!

★

What has 100 feet but can't walk?

A dead centipede!

★

What do old fish wear?

Shawls!

Which profession gets the most fringe benefits ?

Hairdressers !

★

In which job do you get the most perks ?

Working in a coffee shop !

★

What runs all day but is never short of breath ?

A train !

★

What is the only thing higher than a king ?

His crown !

★

What sort of eggs go into uncharted areas of the world ?

Egg - splorers !

What is a volcano ?

A headless mountain !

★

What do you call an American dentist ?

A Yank !

★

Why don't elephants believe in fairy stories ?

They don't believe in mumbo - jumbo !

★

What's the difference between a blue elephant and an apple ?

Apples aren't blue !

★

What is huge, grey and has 12 feet ?

Three elephants !

What driver has never passed a test ?

A screwdriver !

★

What is the biggest mouse ever discovered ?

The hippopotamouse !

★

Why did the idiot drive his car off the side of a mountain ?

Because someone told him that it was fitted with air brakes !

Why did the idiot racing driver make 10 pitstops during a race ?

He was asking for directions !

★

What did the clean dog say to the dirty dog ?

Long time no flea !

★

What do you give a monster with big feet ?

Big shoes !

★

What sort of holidays do cannibals never go on ?

Self-catering !

★

How do worms drive birds crazy ?

By sleeping late - and never being the early bird !

What do you call a rabbit's pram ?

A buns buggy !

★

What do you get if you cross a giant monster with a frog ?

Something that can catch aeroplanes with its tongue !

★

What does a frog do when it dies ?

It croaks !

★

What sort of shoes do frogs wear in summer ?

Open-toad sandals !

★

Why did the cannibal have indigestion ?

He must have eaten someone who disagreed with him !

What did one sardine say to the other sardine when he saw a submarine full of people ?

"You'll never get me into one of those things !"

★

A woman went into a pet shop and asked if she could have a hamster for her son.

"Sorry," replied the shop keeper, "we don't do part exchange !"

★

Why do ghosts go to the shops during the sales ?

They enjoy bargain haunting !

What does a vegetarian cannibal eat ?

Swedes !

★

Did you hear about the guard dog that loved raw onions and garlic ?

His bark was much, much worse than his bite !

★

Did you hear about the cowboy who only wore one spur ?

He wanted his horse to run round in circles !

★

My friend is so stupid that he thinks twice before saying nothing !

★

This garden is very light !

Yes, that's because I planted a lot of bulbs last year !

A man was eating when a little dog came along and started biting his trouser leg. He looked at the owner of the dog, who was doing nothing about this, and asked if it was all right to throw it a bit.

"Of course you can throw it a bit !" replied the owner.

The man picked up the dog and threw it over a fence into a pond !

★

Let me tell you the joke about the mind reader...

...what do you mean you've already heard it ?

★

I went to the ghostly circus last night - to see the fright rope walker !

★

Did you hear about the man who ran away with a deer to get married ?

They anteloped !

Why did Arnie take a grenade launcher to a birthday party ?

Because someone told him he would have to blow up the balloons !

★

The bionic android told his doctor that he thought he was going mad !

The doctor examined him, and agreed. "You've got a screw loose alright !"

A man rescued a vampire from drowning, and the vampire bit him as soon as they got onto dry land.

The man said, "If that's all the fangs I get, I'll let you drown next time !"

★

How did the featherweight boxer do in his last fight ?

He tickled his opponent until he gave in !

★

What does a skeleton eat at a fast food restaurant ?

Ribs !

★

What do you call an elephant wearing rubber boots ?

A wellyphant !

★

What time did your wristwatch stop ?

I don't know, I wasn't looking !

I like the simple things in life !

Wow, you'll love my sister !

"Would you say your sister was pretty or ugly ?"

"Both !"

"How can she be both ?"

"She's pretty ugly !"

★

My wife thinks she's a door
- I think she's just a bit unhinged !

How do you keep an idiot entertained
for hours on end ?

Just give him a piece of paper with
'PLEASE TURN OVER' written on both sides !

★

Which knight designed tombs ?

Sir Cophagus !

★

Which famous artist invented fizzy drinks ?

Lemonado Da Vinci !

★

Doctor, doctor, I've got a button stuck up my nose,
what should I do ?

Breathe through the four little holes !

★

First cat -Where do fleas go in the winter ?

Second cat - Search me !

What do bees do when they move into a new hive ?

They have a house swarming party !

★

What do you call a woman with a chimney on her head ?

Ruth !

★

Where is the easiest place to find diamonds ?

In a pack of cards !

★

The opera singer's voice filled the hall – and then emptied it !

★

"Mum, please may we make mud pies ?"

"Yes, dear, but remember to wash your hands before you eat them !"

Why do vampires like funerals ?

Because every shroud has a silver lining !

★

What sport did Frankenstein's monster compete in ?

The pole volt !

★

What do you give a sick snake ?

Asp - rin !

★

Williamson, you asked for the afternoon off yesterday to go and see your doctor but I saw you going into the cinema with a friend !"

"The doctor is my friend !"

★

"I got a puncture driving here today !"

"I told you to watch out for that fork in the road !"

My dog saw a sign that said "wet paint", and so he did just that !

Did you hear about the idiot who simply couldn't do decimals - for some reason he could never see the point !

★

What did the curtain say to the window ?

"I've got you covered !"

★

Why do cows lie down when it rains ?

To keep each udder dry !

What did the big chimney say to the little chimney ?

"You're far too young to smoke !"

★

Dumb Dan was given the job of painting the college flagpole, but he didn't know how to work out how much paint he would need.

"Lay it on the floor and measure it," suggested a friend.

"Don't be stupid," replied Dan, "I need to know the height, not the length !"

★

My dog is a real problem. He chases everything and anything on a bike ! I don't know what to do !

Just take his bike away !

★

What did one virus say to the other virus?

"Stay away, I think I've got penicillin !"

Why are vampires good comedians ?

They have a biting wit !

★

Why did the idiot take his windows to the shop ?

He wanted them measured for new curtains !

★

My son has just been accepted by a medical school...but they don't want him while he's alive !

Caroline just got fired. She worked for eight hours a day and she slept for eight hours a day.

Unfortunately they were the same eight hours !

★

What do dogs and trees have in common ?

Bark !

★

What do plumbers like to do in the garden ?

Plant leeks !

★

How does a witch tell the time ?

With a witch-watch !

★

How do you hire a car ?

Take the wheels off and stand it on some bricks !

Why was the surgeon working on the road?

It needed a by-pass!

★

What do you call an alien with two heads?

A two-headed alien!

★

What do aliens do with humans they find in spaceships?

Put them in the cupboard - they like to keep tinned food for emergencies!

What should you do if you find a green alien?

Wait until it's ripe!

★

What lights do aliens switch on when it's dark?

Satellites!

★

Where do aliens live?

In greenhouses!

★

What do evil aliens eat for lunch?

Human beings on toast!

★

What do aliens have to do before they can drive a rocket at twice the speed of light in deep space?

Reverse it out of the garage!

Why was the robot rubbing its joints with a DVD ?

Because it was a DVD of Grease !

★

Why do steel robots have so many friends ?

Because they have magnetic personalities !

★

What has four eyes and a mouth ?

The Mississippi !

★

Did you hear about the cement truck
that crashed into the prison bus ?

They ended up with a bunch of hardened criminals !

★

Did you hear about the ship carrying red paint that
crashed into a ship carrying blue paint ?

The passengers were marooned !

What game do aliens play to while away
the hours in deep space ?

Moonopoly !

★

How do you know when aliens are jealous ?

Easy – they turn green !

★

How do you contact someone who lives on Saturn ?

Give them a ring !

★

What is the quickest way to get an alien baby to sleep ?

Rocket !

What is the name of the planet inhabited by video recorders ?

Planet of the Tapes !

★

What ticket do you ask for to go there for a holiday ?

Return to the Planet of the Tapes !

★

Which side of a spaceship passes closest to the planets ?

The outside !

★

Where do aliens keep fish they capture from other planets ?

In a planetarium !

★

What do you call a sad spaceship ?

An unidentified crying object !

ALIEN SCHOOL REPORT

Music	He loves the Planet Suite by Holst !
Chemistry	Blew off one of his heads making rocket fuel !
Martian	KLargin SCRungjlkfr TTTTugt FRelOOmmMw~We TTrRaaakk !
Maths	Can count up to 17 using the fingers on his left hand !

★

Why are aliens good for the environment ?

Because they are green !

What is worse than finding a 12 legged Venusian
mega - maggot in your apple ?

**Finding half a 12 legged Venusian
mega - maggot in your apple !**

★

Doctor, doctor, I've just swallowed a clock!

Don't worry - there's no cause for alarm !

★

Doctor, doctor, I keep thinking I'm a pair of curtains !

Pull yourself together!

★

Doctor, can you give me something for my kidneys ?

How about a few rashers of bacon ?

★

Doctor, doctor, everyone keeps ignoring me !

Next, please !

Doctor, doctor, I keep thinking I'm a bee.

Buzz off, can't you see I'm busy !

★

Doctor, doctor, I've broken my arm in two places.

Well don't go back there again !

★

Doctor, doctor, my husband smells like fish.

Poor sole !

★

Doctor, doctor, I get a pain in the eye
every time I drink coffee.

Have you tried taking the spoon out ?

★

Doctor - You seem to be in excellent health.
Your pulse is as regular as clockwork.

Patient -That's because you've got your hand on my watch !

Doctor, doctor, when I press with my finger here...it hurts, and here...it hurts, and here...and here...What do you think is wrong with me?

You have a broken finger!

★

Doctor, doctor, I've lost my memory.

When did this happen ?

When did what happen ?

★

Doctor, doctor, I keep thinking I'm a caterpillar.

Don't worry you'll soon change !

★

Doctor, doctor, I've had stomach ache since I ate three crabs yesterday.

Did they smell bad when you took them out of their shells ?

What do you mean 'took them out of their shells' ?

Doctor, doctor, I feel like a dog.

Lie down!

★

Doctor, doctor, I keep thinking I'm a spider!

What a web of lies!

★

What did the teacher give the alien monster for lunch?

Class 4B!

★

What sort of music do robots like best?

Steel band music!

★

How do you invite a robot to a party?

Send round a tinvitation!

Where do alien children go in the evenings ?

Rocket and roll concerts !

★

What are wealthy aliens members of ?

The jet set !

★

Why do aliens have seven fingers on each hand ?

Because otherwise they would have two empty fingers in each glove !

★

How do you know when an alien is homesick ?

He just moons about all over the place !

★

What do you give a sick alien ?

Planetcetamol !

What do you call a poster advertising
the last teddy for sale ?

A one ted poster !

★

What goes zzub, zzub ?

A bee flying backwards !

★

My brother got thrown out of the zoo
for feeding the monkeys.

He fed them to the lions !

★

What do you get when you cross an
elephant with a mouse ?

Huge holes in the skirting boards !

★

What does an alien gardener do with his hedges ?

Eclipse them every spring !

Why are vampires always cheerful ?

Because they are terrified of being cross !

★

1 in 5 people in the world are Chinese and there are
5 people in my family – so one of them must be Chinese !
It's either my mum or my dad...
Or my older brother Stephen...
Or my younger brother Chen-Jun-Hsing...
But I think it's Stephen !

★

What do monsters' children do at Halloween ?

They go from door to door dressed as humans !

★

What's the hardest key to turn ?

A donkey !

★

What do you call a sleeping bull ?

A bulldozer !

Man – Doctor, doctor, I feel so tired I don't know where I am half the time.

Dentist - Open wide !

★

Doctor, doctor, I think I'm a spoon.

Just sit still and don't stir !

★

Doctor, doctor, I think I'm a bridge.

What's come over you ?

So far, three cars, a bus and a motorcycle!

★

Doctor, doctor, I'm going to die in 51 seconds!

I will be with you in a minute !

★

Doctor, doctor, I think I'm a needle !

I see your point !

MAD MISCELLANY

What does Doctor Jeckyll do on holiday ?

He tans his Hyde !

★

How can you tell if a computer is upset ?

It will have a chip on its shoulder !

★

Which Russian leader was round and purple ?

Alexander the Grape !

★

What will you get if you swallow plutonium ?

Atomic ache !

★

Have you put some more water in the goldfish bowl ?

No, it hasn't drunk the water I put in six months ago yet !

What is a bunsen burner for?

Setting fire to bunsens?

★

Why did the boy go to boarding school?

Because he was always bored!

★

The meat in our school cafeteria is really tough it challenged me to a fight after school!

He is the sort of man that girls look at twice - they can't believe he is so ugly the first time !

★

How does an idiot get to the top of a tree ?

Stands on an acorn and waits for it to grow !

★

What do baby fish eat on their birthday ?

Fish cakes !

★

What do frogs drink at bedtime ?

Croako !

★

What kind of fish is useful when it's icy ?

Skate !

Do old car tyres get retired?

★

What do you call a fish with no eyes?

Fsh!

★

Roses are red
Violets are blue
You look like a codfish
And smell like one too!

★

Why was the fish so happy?

Because he was moving to a new plaice!

Where do little fish go every morning ?

To plaice school !

★

How could the dolphin afford to buy a house ?

He prawned everything !

★

Why did the whale cross the road ?

To get to the other tide !

★

What happened to the shark who swallowed a bunch of keys ?

He got lockjaw !

★

Knock, knock...
Who's there ?
Cod...
Cod who ?
Cod a minute to spare ?

Knock, knock...
Who's there?
Plaice...
Plaice who?
Plaice to see you!

★

Knock, knock...
Who's there?
Haddock...
Haddock who?
Haddock 'nuff of this – I'm off!

★

How do fish go into business?

They start on a small scale!

Knock, knock...
Who's there ?
Eel...
Eel who ?
Eel be here in a minute - open the door !

★

Knock, knock...
Who's there ?
Crab...
Crab who ?
Crab the door handle and pull !

★

Knock, knock...
Who's there ?
I'm sturgeon...
I'm sturgeon who ?
I'm sturgeon you to open the door !

★

Knock, knock...
Who's there ?
Whale...
Whale who ?
Whale meet again !

Knock, knock...
Who's there ?
Dolphin...
Dolphin who ?
Dolphin you can get away with this !

★

Knock, knock...
Who's there ?
Distress
Distress who ?
Distress is brand new !

★

Knock, knock...
Who's there ?
Lobster...
Lobster who ?
Lobster key out through the window and I'll open it !

Knock, knock...
Who's there ?
Al Kipper...
Al Kipper who ?
Al Kipper few days here if that's OK !

★

Knock, knock...
Who's there ?
Minnow...
Minnow who ?
Minnow you're in there !

★

Knock, knock...
Who's there ?
The seaweed...
The seaweed who ?
The seaweed, so I need to come in and get dry !

★

Knock, knock...
Who's there ?
Trout...
Trout who ?
Trout the day I've been waiting here !

Knock, knock...
Who's there ?
Wave...
Wave who ?
Wave got tired of waiting – we're off !

★

Knock, knock...
Who's there ?
Piranha...
Piranha who ?
Piranha kettle and we'll have a nice cup of tea !

★

Knock, knock...
Who's there ?
Whale...
Whale who ?
Whale have a different sort of joke now...

How do mummies hide ?

They wear masking tape !

★

Who is the strongest man in the world ?

A policeman - he can hold up a whole street full of traffic with one hand !

★

What part of your body is curry good for ?

Your tikka !

★

What do you get if you cross a cat with a canary ?

A peeping tom !

★

What is the name of the detective that Shakespeare invented ?

Shylock Holmes !

What do you call a bear without a beard ?

Bare-faced !

★

What happened when the piano fell on the army barracks ?

There was A flat Major !

★

What time is it when you're hungry ?

Time to get something to eat !

★

What came between the Iron Age and the Stone Age ?

The cabb - age !

★

What do you call a mad squirrel ?

Nuts !

What did the rabbit say when it went bald?

Hare today, gone tomorrow!

★

What does a girl say when she's going out with a bear?

We're going teddy!

★

How can you send a liquid through the post?

Dip a letter in a cup of tea!

What is big and grey and wobbly ?

A jellyphant !

★

Why was the pop group thrown out of the nightclub by the bouncer ?

They were an elastic band !

★

What wears a sock on its bottom ?

Your leg !

★

What do you call a snowman in the summer ?

A puddle !

★

What is the only thing you can have in an empty pocket ?

A hole !

What sort of music do very, very cold people listen to ?

The blues !

★

Waiter - There's a dead mouse in my salad !

It's the terrible food in this place that kills them, Sir !

★

Waiter - What are these two worms on my plate ?

They're the sausages, sir !

A robber who stole three thousand bars of soap, has made a clean getaway!

★

Why did the elephant refuse to play cards with his two friends?

Because one of them was lion and the other was a cheetah!

★

How do you stop moles from digging up your lawn?

Lock the toolshed!

★

What's black and white and wet at the bottom?

A nun paddling in the sea!

★

How does the queen of the sea travel around her kingdom?

By octobus!

Why are ducks so miserable ?

They always have down in the mouth !

★

What goes oom, oom, oom ?

A cow walking backwards !

★

Waiter, there's half a dead cockroach
in my food !

You'll have to pay for the half
you've eaten, Sir !

★

What sort of crossword clues does Dracula like ?

Cryptic ones !

★

Mary had a little lamb,
She ate it with mint sauce !
If she buys a jar of mustard,
I'd watch out, mister horse !

How do you make a sausage roll?

Push it down a hill!

★

Why do bees buzz?

Because they can never remember the words!

★

How do you know when a dog is house trained?

It leaves its little poodles outside!

★

What is an alien's favourite movie?

Starzan!

Why is the leopard the only animal
that can't hide from hunters ?

Because it's always spotted !

★

Four kippers please, and leave the eyes in
- I'll need something to see me through the week !

★

Why was the ugly monster called Isaiah ?

Because he had one eye higher than the other !

Where are school dinners served ?

The mushroom !

★

With alphabet soup,
you can spell your name,
you can write rude words,
again and again.
With alphabet soup,
take it or leave it,
whatever you spell,
you'll have to eat it !

★

How do you survive an electric shock ?

Call the operator and ask them to reverse the charge !

★

What building drips cheese and tomatoes onto the town beneath ?

The leaning tower of Pizza !

A young man was sitting by the fire watching the kettle boil...

"If only we could harness this wonderful power of steam, perhaps one day we could even use it to drive vehicles and carry people from one town to another..."

His mother called out to him...

"Hurry up and get dressed or you'll miss the train to work again!"

★

Where is the best place to keep a pie?

Your tummy!

Why couldn't Noah, his son and his wife all go fishing ?

He only had two worms !

★

Did you hear about the orchestra leader who survived being hit by lightning ? Fortunately he was a very bad conductor !

★

What is green and hot and goes round and round ?

An alien in a tumble drier !

★

Did you hear about the stupid robber ?

He threw a brick through the jewellers' window on Monday night, and then came back and did the same again on Tuesday night – someone told him that the window had double glazing !

How do you get directions in deep space?

Askeroid!

★

What sort of bird can see round corners?

A crane!

★

Doctor, doctor, my wife thinks she's a jumbo jet!

Don't be silly - she isn't even an elephant!

What do bad comedians eat at breakfast ?

Corny flakes !

★

Why did the alien turn the restaurant waiter upside down ?

Someone told him that you had to tip the waiter !

★

What are round and pink and wear trainers ?

Jogging bottoms !

★

Why did the witch put her broomstick in the fridge ?

She fancied a cold spell !

★

How do fish travel on holiday ?

By whale way !

How do cavemen get to know each other ?

By joining clubs !

★

What do you call frozen mice ?

Micicles !

★

Doctor, doctor, my little boy has swallowed my wristwatch !

Don't worry, we will soon see the passage of time !

★

What shall I do with all this soil I've got after digging this hole ?

Just dig another hole and bury it !

★

How do you keep an idiot in suspense ?

I'll tell you on page 2890 !

What did the maths teacher do when his nose got blocked?

He worked it out with his pencil and ruler!

★

What do you call a wizard on a broomstick?

A flying sorcerer!

★

Did you hear about the man who slept under a tractor?

He wanted to wake up oily in the morning!

Why were the carpenter's teeth chipped ?

Because he was always biting his nails !

★

What did the vampire doctor say ?

Necks please !

★

Two oranges were playing tennis, the score was 40-40; what did the umpire shout ?

Juice !

★

Why does Dracula never intend to get married ?

He is a bat - chelor !

What happened to the football that was kicked close to a fan?

It blew out of the stadium!

★

What sort of car does an alligator drive?

Some old crock!

★

What job did the spider get?

He was a web designer!

★

What do you get if you cross a warlock and a PC?

A computer wizard!

★

What do you get if you cross a dinosaur with a fish?

Jurassic shark!

What does an Italian pirate's parrot say ?

Pizzas of eight, pizzas of eight !

★

When Mary had a little lamb,
the doctor was surprised,
but when Old Macdonald had a farm,
he just couldn't believe his eyes !

★

Little Jack Horner,
sat in the corner,
eating his Christmas pie.
Along came a spider,
and sat down beside him,
and said "I think I'm in the wrong poem here !"

What do cannibals do at a wedding ?

Toast the bridesmaids !

★

What sort of jungle animal works on the railways ?

A railway lion !

★

What is the best time of year to pick apples and pears ?

When the farmer is away on holiday !

★

What pen does a hairless man use ?

A bald point !

★

Where are you allowed to eat toffees ?

On a chew - chew train !

Where do cats sleep ?

On a caterpillar !

★

Why should you always laugh when a vampire tells you a joke ?

Because they like people to get the point !

★

What sort of posters do naughty teddies find themselves on ?

Wan - ted posters !

What do you get out of a poorly piano?

A sick note!

★

Where does Tarzan buy his clothes?

At a jungle sale!

★

Where does Tarzan the vampire bite people?

In the jungular!

★

Why was Dr Frankenstein never lonely?

Because he was good at making new friends!

★

Where does Tarzan buy his loincloths?

From an end-of-loin sale!

What did the man say when he walked into the bar ?

OOF ! (It was a metal bar !)

★

Why can't pigs ever get a good radio or TV signal ?

There's always too much crackling !

★

Why did the idiot come top of the class at school ?

He was the only one who passed the dope test !

★

What do you find in an angry sewing machine ?

Cross stitches !

What fish went to music college ?

The piano tuna !

★

What do you call a boy made of crisp packets?

Russell !

★

What exams do wizards do at school ?

Spelling !

★

What do you call a vampire's handkerchief ?

A neckerchief !

★

What sort of vampires are interested in sport ?

Football fangs !

What do you call a vampire who wears a raincoat ?

Count Macula !

★

What do you call a vampire who lives in a suitcase ?

Count Packula !

★

What do you call a vampire who likes doing housework ?

Count Vac - ula !

★

What do you call a vampire who eats nails ?

Count Tackula !

★

What do you call a vampire who wakes you up to go to school ?

Count Draculalarm !

What do you call a vampire who eats cakes all day ?

Count Dracutart !

★

Why did the idiot throw a bucket of water into the wardrobe ?

Someone told him there was a smoking jacket in there !

★

How did the vegetable escape being eaten by a dog ?

It was a marrow escape !

★

Why is the school orchestra in China ?

Because they made the mistake of asking if the audience had any requests !

★

What is white, scary and soft ?

A jellyton !

What is white, scary and swims round in the sea ?

A skellyfish !

★

Why is the man with the photographic memory so miserable ?

He has negative thoughts !

★

What is a skeleton ?

Bones with the person taken off !

★

How do you know if there is an alien in your house ?

There will be a spaceship parked in your garden !

★

How do you communicate with aliens out in deep space ?

You have to shout really, really loudly !

How do you catch a Venusian mega mouse?

In a Venusian mega mouse-trap!

★

What do evil aliens grind up to make a hot drink?

Coffee beings!

★

If you get lost in space - who should
you ask for directions?

An alien hairdresser -
they know all the short cuts!

★

What do you get if you cross a bird with a magician?

A flying sorcerer!

★

What do you get if you cross a centipede
with a chicken?

Enough drumsticks to feed an army!

What is the most popular sentence at school ?

"I don't know !"

★

What do you call a snowman in the Tropics?

Lost !

★

Which is heavier - the full moon or the half moon ?

The half moon because the full moon is lighter !

★

How many balls of string would you
need to reach the moon ?

Just one if it's long enough !

★

Did you hear about the man who thought he was a
snooker ball. ?

He always went to the end of the queue !

WHAT DO YOU CALL ...

What do you call a person made of rubber who stands by the door of a nightclub ?

A bouncer !

★

What do you call a vampire swing singer ?

Fang Sinatra !

★

What do you call a German man wearing a motorcycle hat ?

Helmut !

★

What do you call a bird that goes to college ?

Polly technic !

★

What do you call a rodent's favourite meal ?

Ratatouille !

What do you call a woman who juggles pints of beer?

Beertrix!

★

What do you call a singing fish?

A sole singer!

★

What do you call a pony with a sore throat?

A little hoarse!

What do you call a woman with a parrot on her head?

Polly!

★

What do you call a woman who works as a bodyguard?

Sal - a - minder!

★

What do you call a woman with a white face?

Blanche!

What do you say to a man who lives just around the corner?

That's Andy!

★

What do you call a duck that lives in a teapot?

A quackpot!

★

What do you call a rodent with a sword?

A mouseketeer!

★

What do you call a sloth's favourite drink?

Ice cream slowda!

★

What do you call a camel with three humps?

Hump-frey!

What do you call a smelly giant gorilla ?

King Pong !

★

What do you call an expensive car for butchers ?

A sausage Rolls !

★

What do you call a dog that likes doing puzzles ?

A lab-rynth !

★

What do you call a man who never pays
for his food ?

Bill !

★

What do you call a dog that wears shorts ?

A Boxer !

What do you call a snake with a pocket calculator?

An adder!

★

What do you call the jewels that ghosts wear?

Tomb stones!

★

What do you call a pig with fangs?

A hampire!

What do you call a pig that acts in Shakespeare plays ?

Hamlet !

★

What do you call a woman who has lots of men at her feet ?

A chiropodist !

★

What do you call the eating implements used by karate club members ?

Chop sticks !

★

What do you call a mushroom who has lots of fun at parties ?

A fungi !

★

What do you call a vicar on a motorbike ?

Rev !

What do you call a dog that can operate a farmer's four-wheel drive car?

A land rover!

★

What do you call Long John Silver's younger brother?

Short John Silver!

★

What do you call a ghostly teddy bear?

Haun-ted!

What do you call a pale teddy bear ?

Wan-ted !

★

What do you call a sun-tanned teddy bear ?

Unwan-ted !

★

What do you call a sweet smelling teddy bear ?

Scen-ted !

★

What do you call a rock climbing teddy bear ?

Moun-ted !

What do you call a teddy bear that's been knocked down by a car ?

Den-ted !

★

What do you call a happy teddy bear ?

Conten-ted !

★

What do you call a teddy bear left at the altar ?

Jil-ted !

★

What do you call a teddy bear that serves in Parliament ?

Elec-ted !

★

What do you call the instruments made from people's insides that monsters play ?

Organs !

What does a whale call the youngest member of the family ?

Her baby blubber !

★

What do you call two rows of cabbages ?

A dual cabbageway !

★

What do you call a worm rich enough to buy a fur jacket ?

A caterpillar !

★

What do you call a wig for a rabbit ?

A harepiece !

★

What do you call a popular person who stays out in the sun for far too long ?

The toast of the town !

What do you call a teacher who makes fireworks?

A head banger!

★

What do you call the person who delivers mail to a soccer club?

The goal - post - man!

★

What do you call a telephone call from one vicar to another?

A parson to parson call!

What do you call an owl that robs the rich
and gives to the poor ?

Robin Hoot !

★

What do you call the stuff that space aliens
put on their cakes ?

Starzipan !

What do you call a homeless snail ?

A slug !

★

What do you call the very earliest spaceship ?

A dinosaucer !

★

What do you call the woman who fell
off the cliff ?

Eileen Dover !

★

What do you call the man walking on
dried leaves ?

Russell !

★

What do you call a man who can't swim ?

Bob !

What do you call a woman who walks around lost ?

Wanda !

★

What do you call a vegetable that goes camping ?

A boy sprout !

★

What do you call an embarrassed potato ?

A beetroot !

★

What do you call the job of making nun's clothes ?

Habit-forming !

What do you call a a lorry full of feet ?

A toe truck !

★

What do you call a snake that crushes wild pigs ?

A boar constrictor !

★

What do you call an older member of your family who thinks he's a pen ?

Your Bic brother !

★

What do you call a film about wildfowl ?

A duckumentary !

★

What do you call a vampire's favourite pudding ?

Leeches and scream !

What do you call a goat's favourite food?

Alphabutt soup!

★

What do you call a cross between a dog and a phone?

A golden receiver!

★

What do you call the place where baby monkeys sleep?

An apricot!

★

What do you call a buffalo that you
can wash your hands in?

A bison!

★

What do you call a deer that goes
out in bad weather?

A rain-deer!

What do you call a place where cats and dogs go to get new tails?

A retailer!

★

What do you call a Russian gardener?

Ivanhoe!

★

What do you call a common alien dog?

A moon-grel!

What do you call a horse that a monster eats at 3 a.m. ?

A nightmare !

★

What do you call the leader of a convent who conquers the World ?

Attila the Nun !

★

What do you call a bird that loves to play cowboys ?

Wyatt Chirp !

★

What do you call the flying machines invented by mummies ?

Pharaohplanes !

★

What do you call it when cannibals eat a comedian ?

A feast of fun !

What do you call a man who steals things?

Rob!

★

What do you call a place where you can rent out Dracula?

A vamp-hire shop!

★

What do you call a noisy alien party?

A space racket!

What do you call a dog that keeps making a bolt for the door ?

Blacksmith !

★

What do you call the event that undertakers and their ponies go to each year ?

The Hearse of the Year Show !

★

What do you call the method of transport used on the sea bed ?

Taxi - crab !

★

What do you call it when you flush a lot ?

A chain reaction !

★

What do you call a pig driving a car ?

Road hog !

What do you call the bird that brings monster babies ?

Frankenstork !

★

What do you call a frog that allows you to park your car ?

A parking Kermit !

★

What do you call a short-legged tramp ?

A low-down bum !

★

What do you call the first part of a robot teacher's schoolday ?

Assembly !

★

What do you call an intelligent insect ?

A spelling bee !

What do you call a TV programme set round a breakfast table ?

A cereal !

★

What do you call something with eight 8 legs and a terrible voice ?

The school choir !

★

What do you call a water otter ?

A kettle !

★

What do you call a computer-operated sheep ?

A ram !

★

What do you call a cat that chases outlaws ?

Posse !

What do you call the place where cats get on the coach?

The puss stop!

★

What do you call a lazy man in a bakery?

A loafer!

★

What do you call it when you shoot at the alarm clock?

Killing time!

What do you call a ghost who haunts TV shows ?

The Phantom of the Oprah !

★

What do you call a woman who spends all her time in the bookmakers ?

Bette !

★

What do you call a car that acts in adventure films ?

Harrison Ford !

★

What do you call the worst player in the school football team ?

The drawback !

★

What do you call a crocodile's favourite card game ?

Snap !

What do you call the nuts that fly around in space?

Astronuts!

★

What do you call a ghost that is a member of the British royal family?

The Prince of Wails!

★

What do you call a liquid that can never freeze?

Hot water!

What do you call a baby crab ?

A nipper !

★

What do you call an adventurous skeleton ?

Indiana Bones !

★

What do you call the teacher with no legs, arms or body ?

The Head !

★

What do you call a man with two left feet ?

Whatever you like - if he tries to catch you he'll just run round in circles !

★

What do you call a bee who is always complaining ?

A grumble bee !

What do you call a man whose father was a Canon ?

A son of a gun !

★

What would you call a friend who had an elephant on his head ?

A flatmate !

★

What do you call a dentist in the army ?

A Drill Sergeant !

What do you call a weekly television programme about people getting washed?

A soap opera!

★

What do you call the man who went to a fancy dress party as a sandwich?

Roland Butter!

★

What do you call a parrot when it has dried itself after a bath?

Polly unsaturated!

★

What do you call an assistant headteacher who thinks he's a cowboy?

The Deputy Head!

What do you call a man who rescues drowning spooks from the sea?

A ghost guard!

★

What do you call King Midas when he stars in a James Bond film?

Goldfinger!

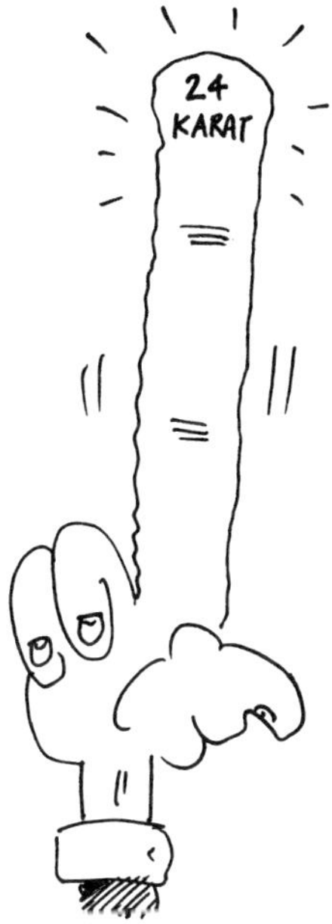

★

What do you call someone who makes half-size models of fish?

A scale modeller!

★

What do you call someone who draws funny pictures of motor vehicles?

A car - toonist!

What do you call the owner of a tool factory?

The Vice Chairman!

★

What do you call a man who drills holes in teapots?

A potholer!

★

What do you call a musical instrument that is played by two teams of twenty people?

A piano forte!

What do you call a kangaroo at the North Pole?

A lost-ralian!

★

What do you call a group of cars?

A clutch!

★

What do you call a puzzle that is so hard it makes people swear?

A crossword!

★

What do you call a teacher who corrects schoolwork?

Mark!

★

What do you call a dinosaur with no eyes?

Do-you-think-he-saurus!

What do you call an elephant that has had too much to drink ?

Trunk !

★

What do you call a fish on a motorcycle ?

A motor pike !

★

What do you call a pen with no hair ?

A bald point !

What do you call the place where parrots make films ?

Pollywood !

★

What do you call a brilliant painting done by a rat ?

A mouseterpiece !

★

What do you call a chicken that eats cement ?

A bricklayer !

★

What do you call a fight between film actors ?

Star Wars !

★

What do you call a cat that has eaten a duck ?

A duck-filled fatty puss !

What do you call a man with a car on his head?

Jack!

★

What do you call a very popular perfume?

A best - smeller!

★

What do you call a rabbit dressed up as a cake?

A cream bun!

CRAZY CROSSES

What do you get if you cross an artist
with a policeman?

A brush with the law!

★

What do you get if you cross a pig
with a centipede?

Bacon and legs!

★

What do you get if you cross a kangaroo with
a skyscraper?

A high jumper!

What do you get if you cross a sheep and a spaceship ?

Apollo neck woolly jumper !

★

What do you get if you cross an overweight golfer and a pair of very tight trousers ?

A hole in one !

★

What do you get if you cross a plumber with a field of cow pats ?

The Pooed Piper !

★

What do you get if you cross an elephant and a bottle of whisky ?

Trunk and disorderly !

★

What do you get if you cross a snowman and a shark ?

Frostbite !

What do you get if you cross a flock of sheep and a radiator?

Central bleating!

★

What do you get if you cross a skunk and a pair of tennis tennis bats?

Ping pong!

★

What do you get if you cross a bear with a freezer?

A teddy brrrrrr!

What do you get if you cross a pair of dogs with a hairdresser ?

A shampoodle and setter !

★

What do you get if you cross a dinosaur with a dog ?

Tyrannosaurus Rex !

★

What do you get if you cross a pudding and a cow pat ?

A smelly jelly !

What do you get if you cross a computer with a vampire?

Something new fangled!

★

What do you get if you cross a tin opener, a vampire and a cricket team?

An opening bat!

★

What do you get if you cross a cow with a grass cutter?

A lawn - mooer!

★

What do you get if you cross an ice cream with a dog?

Frost - bite!

What do you get if you cross a mouse
and a bottle of olive oil?

A squeak that oils itself!

★

What do you get if you cross a helicopter
with a pasty?

Pie in the sky!

★

What do you get if you cross a bag with a mallard?

A ducksack!

What do you get if you cross a hat with a field of cows?

A pat on the head!

★

What do you get if you cross a large computer with a beefburger?

A Big Mac!

★

What do you get if you cross an overheating large computer with a beefburger?

A Big Mac and fries!

★

What do you get if you cross a pig and a part in a film?

A ham roll!

What do you get if you cross a bike and a rose?

Bicycle petals!

★

What do you get if you cross a jogger with a pie?

Puff pastry!

★

What do you get if you cross a detective with a cat?

A peeping tom!

What do you get if you cross a dog with a vampire ?

A were - woof !

★

What do you get if you cross a toadstool and a full suitcase ?

Not mushroom for your holiday clothes !

★

What do you get if you cross a TV programme and a load of sheep ?

A flock - u - mentary !

What do you get if you cross a sports reporter with a vegetable?

A common - tater!

★

What do you get if you cross a chicken and an electricity socket?

A battery hen!

★

What do you get if you cross a plank of wood with a pencil?

A drawing board!

What do you get if you cross a wireless with a hairdresser ?

Radio waves !

★

What do you get if you cross a hairdresser and a bucket of cement ?

Permanent waves !

★

What do you get if you cross a tortoise and a storm ?

A not - in - a - hurry - cane !

What do you get if you cross an alligator and King Midas?

A croc of gold!

★

What do you get if you cross a chicken with a pod?

Chickpeas!

★

What do you get if you cross a frog with a traffic warden?

Toad away!

★

What do you get if you cross a cow and a goat?

Butter from a butter!

What do you get if you cross a computer with a potato?

Micro chips!

★

What do you get if you cross a crocodile with a camera?

A snapshot!

★

What do you get if you cross a baby with soldiers?

Infantry!

What do you get if you cross a biscuit with a car tyre?

Crumbs!

★

What do you get if you cross a dog with a football game?

Spot-The-Ball!

★

What do you get if you cross a spider with a computer?

A web page!

★

What do you get if you cross a snake with a building site?

A boa-constructor!

What do you get if you cross a cow with a crystal ball?

A message from the udder side!

★

What do you get if you cross a hedgehog with a giraffe?

A long-necked toothbrush!

★

What do you get if you cross a bottle of washing-up liquid and a mouse?

Bubble and squeak!

What do you get if you cross a mountain and a baby?

A cry for Alp!

★

What do you get if you cross a vampire and a circus entertainer?

Something that goes straight for the juggler!

What do you get if you cross a cow with an out of date map ?

Udderly lost !

★

What do you get if you cross a fish and bad breath ?

Halibut - osis !

★

What do you get if you cross a flea with some moon rock ?

A lunar - tick !

What do you get if you cross a bunch of flowers with some insects?

Ants in your plants!

★

What do you get if you cross a very bent piece of wood with a spaceship?

Warp factor 7!

★

What do you get if you cross a compass and a shellfish?

A guided mussel!

What do you get if you cross a bunch of flowers with a burgler ?

A violet robbery !

★

What do you get if you cross a leopard and a bunch of flowers ?

A beauty spot !

★

What do you get if you cross a pub and a steelworks ?

An iron bar !

What do you get if you cross a pen with Napoleon's feet ?

A footnote in history !

★

What do you get if you cross a skunk and a pair of rubber boots ?

Smelly wellies !

★

What do you get if you cross a suitcase with an idiot ?

A nut case !

★

What do you get if you cross the devil with an anagram ?

Santa !

What do you get if you cross a bee and a coach ?

A buzzzzz !

★

What do you get if you cross a monster and a chicken ?

Free strange eggs !

★

What do you get if you cross a Welshman with a problem ?

A Dai - lemma !

★

What do you get if you cross a book and a pound of fat ?

Lard of the Rings !

What do you get if you cross a donkey
and Christmas ?

Muletide greetings !

★

What do you get if you cross a skeleton and a dog ?

An animal that buries itself !

★

What do you get if you cross a chemical and a bicycle ?

Bike carbonate of soda !

★

How do rabbits travel ?

By hareplane !

What do you get if you cross a classroom with a computer supplier ?

Floppy desks !

★

What do you get if you cross a Shakespeare play and three eggs ?

Omelette !

★

What do you get if you cross a Shakespeare play and a pig ?

A Ham omelette !

What do you get if you cross a Shakespeare play and a vampire?

Macbreath!

★

What do you get if you cross a motorcycle and a funny story?

A Yamaha ha ha ha!

★

What do you get if you cross a hairdresser, a storyteller and a young horse?

A pony tail!

What do you get if you cross a cow
and a running machine ?

A milk shake !

★

What do you get if you cross a sheep with a holiday resort ?

The Baaahaaamaaas !

★

What do you get if you cross a sheep and a vampire ?

A were - wool !

What do you get if you cross a newsreader and a toad?

A croaksman!

★

What do you get if you cross a newsreader and a ghost?

A spooksman!

★

What do you get if you cross a vampire and a bowl of soup?

Scream of tomato!

What do you get if you cross a pig and a laundry ?

Hogwash !

★

What do you get if you cross a cake and a disco ?

Abundance !

★

What do you get if you cross an Innuit and an ex-boyfriend ?

The cold shoulder !

What do you get if you cross a
skeleton and a garden spade ?

Skullduggery !

★

What do you get if you cross a skeleton,
a feather and a joke book ?

Rib ticklers !

★

What do you get if you cross a
mad man and a bakery ?

Doughnuts !

What do you get if you cross a skeleton and a tumble drier ?

Bone - dry clothes !

★

What do you get if you cross a giant ape and a self defence class ?

Kong - Fu !

★

What do you get if you cross a pig and an emergency vehicle ?

A hambulance !

What do you get if you cross a gorilla and a prisoner ?

A Kong - vict !

★

What do you get if you cross a vampire and a plumber ?

A drain in the neck !

★

What do you get if you cross a carrier pigeon with a woodpecker ?

A bird that knocks before delivering a message !

★

What do you get if you cross an insect and a dance ?

A cricket ball !

★

What do you get if you cross a vampire with a mummy ?

Something you wouldn't want to unwrap !

What do you get if you cross a mummy and a spaceship ?

Tutankha - moon !

★

What do you get if you cross a frog
and a secret agent ?

A croak and dagger story !

★

What do you get if you cross a jellyfish
and an aircraft ?

A jelly - copter !

★

What do you get if you cross a singer and a ladder ?

Someone who can easily hit the high notes !

★

What do you get if you cross an
Italian landmark and a ghost ?

The screaming tower of Pisa !

ODDS AND ENDS

Knock, knock...
Who's there ?
Alison
Alison who ?
Alison at your keyhole every day !

★

Knock, knock...
Who's there ?
Jaws
Jaws who ?
Jaws truly !

★

Knock, knock...
Who's there ?
Satin
Satin who ?
Satin a chair and it collapsed !

★

Knock, knock...
Who's there ?
Midas
Midas who ?
Midas well open the door and find out !

Knock, knock...
Who's there ?
Renata
Renata who ?
Renata sugar - can I borrow a cup ?

★

Knock, knock...
Who's there ?
Isadore
Isadore who ?
Isadore on the right way round ?

★

Knock, knock...
Who's there ?
Don
Don who ?
Don be afraid...but I think I saw a ghost !

Knock, knock...
Who's there ?
Bert
Bert who ?
Bert you'll never guess !

★

Knock, knock...
Who's there ?
Jemima
Jemima who ?
Jemima coming round for a chat ?

★

Knock, knock...
Who's there ?
Amos
Amos who ?
Amos be going mad - I've come to the wrong house !

★

Knock, knock...
Who's there ?
Caesar
Caesar who ?
Caesar jolly good fellow...

Knock, knock...
Who's there ?
Arthur
Arthur who ?
Arthur minute and I'll show you my ID card !

★

Knock, knock...
Who's there ?
Derek
Derek who ?
Derek get richer and the poor get poorer... !

★

Knock, knock...
Who's there ?
Isaac
Isaac who ?
Isaac you if you don't report into work right now !

Knock, knock...
Who's there ?
Alma
Alma who ?
Alma lone out here - open up !

★

Knock, knock...
Who's there ?
Saul
Saul who ?
Saul the same to me !

★

Knock, knock...
Who's there ?
Stan
Stan who ?
Stan back, I'm going to break down the door !

Knock, knock...
Who's there ?
Belinda
Belinda who ?
Belinda few ingredients together and make a cake !

★

Knock, knock...
Who's there ?
Roman
Roman who ?
Roman roads are always straight !

★

Knock, knock...
Who's there ?
Harpie
Harpie who ?
Harpie holidays !

★

Knock, knock...
Who's there ?
Seth
Seth who ?
Seth this is how you treat your oldest friend !

Knock, Knock...
Who's there ?
Arthur !
Arthur Who ?
Arthur any more biscuits left - I'm still hungry !

★

Knock, knock...
Who's there ?
Eddie
Eddie who ?
Eddie body in dere want by cold ?

★

Knock, knock...
Who's there ?
Theodore
Theodore who ?
Theodore is locked !

★

Knock, knock...
Who's there ?
Woof
Woof who ?
Woof, woof, woof, woof, woof...
(Oh, it's the dog !)

Sardines really are the most stupid fish of all!

Why do you say that?

They lock themselves into little cans, and then leave the key outside!

★

Why did the idiot make a hole in his umbrella?

So that he could tell when it stopped raining!

★

Why are you home from school so early?

I was sent home because my best friend was smoking!

But if your best friend was smoking – why were YOU sent home?

Because I was the one who set him on fire!

★

What kind of coat will keep you warm in winter?

A blazer!

Did you hear about the plastic surgeon who fell asleep in front of the fire and melted ?

★

I think I've got chicken pox !

What makes you think it's chicken pox ?

Because I feel peckish !

★

What did the postage stamp say to the envelope ?

Stick with me and we'll go places !

★

What did the monster have after his parents bought him a saw for his birthday ?

Lots of half brothers and sisters !

★

What is black and white and can't turn round in a narrow space ?

A nun carrying a snooker cue !

Dad, do you have a good memory for faces?

I think so, son, why do you ask?

Because I've just broken your shaving mirror!

★

Mummy, mummy, Charles has broken my favourite doll!

How did he do that?

When I hit him over the head with it!

★

Doctor, I've got double vision!

Well close one eye!

★

Waiter this omelette tastes awful!

Sir, I can assure you that our chef has been making omelettes since he was a child!

That may be true – but can I have one of his fresher ones please?

What is white on the outside, black and green on the inside and slippery when you eat it ?

A slug and lettuce sandwich !

★

What has four legs and flies ?

Two pairs of trousers !

★

Why did the burglar saw the legs off his bed ?

Because he wanted to lie low for a while !

★

Did you hear about the idiot who wrote himself a letter? He forgot to sign it and then when it arrived he couldn't work out who it was from !

★

Who are the rudest creatures in the farmyard ?

Chickens - they are always using fowl language !